Get Known Be Seen

– Volume 1 –

**How to Write Your Book
and Leverage it**

Get Known Be Seen

Compiled by Deborah Fay

Copyright © 2018 MJL Publications

First published 2018

Publisher: MJL Publications
             17 Spencer Avenue
             Deception Bay QLD 4508
             Australia

WEB: www.mjlpublications.com.au

Each of the contributing authors in this book retain the rights to their individual contributions, all of which have been printed as a part of this compilation with their permission. Each author is responsible for any opinions expressed within their own stories.

All rights reserved. Without limiting the rights under copyright reserved above, no part of this publication may be reproduced, stored in or introduced in to a database and retrieval system, or transmitted in any form or by any means (electronic, mechanical, photocopying, recording or otherwise) without the prior written permission of both the owner of the copyright and the above publishers.

ISBN# 978-0-6483778-6-3

Contents

How to Write and Publish a Book 5

Writing is a Huge Part of Being Fully Self-Expressed ... 29

From Coward to Legal Lioness 43

I Am Ria Sarah 61

You Can Leave Your *Heart* On 71

A Passion for Marketing 91

Tragedy and Grit 101

10 Winning Tactics to Market Your Book with Video 119

A Vision to Win 139

The Retail Experiment 151

A Writer's Journey 173

How Writing A Business Book Can Launch Your Personal Brand 189

Who Do I Think I Am to Write A Book? 201

The Accidental Author 219

Leveraging Your Book 233

How to Write and Publish a Book
by Deborah Fay

Why would you write a book? Writing and publishing a book is an exciting and inspired journey for anyone who has ever considered becoming a published author.

Whether you are an aspiring author or a solopreneur looking for a way to raise your profile and take your business to the next level, writing a book is a great way to meet a number of needs.

Perhaps it has been a long-term dream for you to become published. Perhaps it is a means to an end. Perhaps you really want to help people. You might want to build a business around your knowledge and expertise and think writing a book would be a great way to set yourself apart from the crowd, increase your influence and build more meaningful relationships with your ideal clients. Maybe you just love writing, or maybe it is a combination of all of the above.

Whatever your reason for wanting to write a book, it is important to consider: why haven't you already written your book?

Some of the reasons I hear include:

- I wouldn't know what to write
- I don't know how to write a book
- I wouldn't know where to start
- I don't know how to put a book together
- It never occurred to me that I could write a book
- I am not sure I am good enough
- I don't know that I know enough
- Who am I to call myself an author?
- Who would want to read what I write?

In this chapter, I intend to give you a good picture of what is involved in writing and publishing a book, including how to organise your knowledge and lay out the content in a book, all the steps you need to take in order to publish your book, identifying where you will need to get help along the way, what platform to use for your manuscript and what platform to choose for publishing.

Now, you may be wondering why you should listen to me. Who am I, and what do I know about writing and publishing?

My own publishing journey began in 2013 after talking with a friend about how she could build a business around her knowledge and expertise. We had both been on a journey where we had reduced the toxins and allergens from our individual environments and we had both collected a large body of information over a period of many years.

I had suggested to my friend, Lorna, that she build a business helping other mums to reduce the toxins in their homes, and I thought we could collect success stories from the many friends we had made along the way who had also taken this journey. These friends had achieved wonderful results for themselves and their families in the areas of health and childhood development, so we thought this would be a great way to show prospective clients what was possible in their own lives if they engaged Lorna to help them.

When we had collected what we thought were enough stories and put them together into a PDF, I thought it would be interesting to explore the possibilities of creating a printed version.

On the 24th of March 2014, with a lot of help from my son Matthew who is quite brilliant with technology, we launched *Domestic Detox* in eBook and in print version using a print-on-demand platform.

I can't tell you how exciting that ride was. Not only were we now authors, we had helped 13 other people to become published authors too, and that was way more fun than I could have imagined.

After consideration, Lorna chose not to go into the business we'd discussed and explored for her, but I now had a new set of skills and a new way to communicate with the world, so later that year I self-published *6 Keys to Happiness* for myself, which is a comprehensive collection of resilience skills and a guide for anyone living with anxiety, depression and low self-esteem.

Over the following 18 months I put another compilation book together with contributions from 25 different authors, and in April 2016 I published *Parenting A Child on the Spectrum*.

I have published 3 other books since then, and all while working full time as a counsellor, which is important for you to know because you really don't need to take a year off in order to write a book and get it published. You can actually achieve a great deal in a short space of time when you know how to do it.

In January this year, I made the decision to officially register MJL Publications as a business and transition from counselling into full time publishing, and I already have a number of projects in the works.

I am so looking forward to showing aspiring authors and small business people how to get published so that they can make a real difference, so let's get started.

There are 3 important steps you need to take in order to write your book and get published. They are:

1. Start with the end in mind;
2. Use the power of visualisation; and
3. **Plan the work, then work the plan.**

Start with The End in Mind

If you don't start with the end in mind, it is like trying to colour in without any lines.

(i) Setting a launch date right at the very beginning of your author journey is a great way to start. Writing a book is a considerably small, albeit important part of publishing a book so make sure you give yourself plenty of time to complete everything you need to complete. Twelve months is a great timeframe to work within, although a book can be written and published in less time.

(ii) Creating a 3D cover of your book before you start writing is an amazingly powerful thing. A 3D visual of your book cover will inspire you to write and keep writing until the very end. In our minds, it's almost as if the book is complete, and we just have to fill in the gaps with our words. It's powerful.

(iii) Think about how you want to feel when you have finished writing your book and get familiar with those feelings. Setting your feeling intentions will keep you anchored in the particular outcome you want to achieve.

(iv) Think about who you want to impact with your writing. Who do you want to write to? How do you want to impact their lives and their thoughts and their experiences of life?

(v) Think about who you most want to share the moment with when you actually finish your book. Who do you want to have by your side? Who's important enough to you that you want to share that moment with them?

(vi) Where do you want to be when you experience that sense of completion of having published your book? How do you think you might like to celebrate?

These are all important factors in setting the scene for writing your book. Starting with the end in mind helps to create a beautiful *emotional* space that will inspire and motivate you to fulfil your dream and meet the outcome that you have in your heart and mind.

Use the Power of Visualisation

The next thing you need to do is use the power of visualisation. You've already thought about what it's going to feel like when you publish your book and what you want to achieve by doing so. Now, we're going to look at how practicing visualisation can help bring your desired outcome to reality.

Something that we need to be aware of before we embark on this journey is that we all have an identity. We all think of ourselves of as being a certain way or *not* being a certain way.

Creativity is a great example of this.

Some of us were told when we were young that we're not creative, that we aren't arty or very good at drawing, or that we aren't very good at writing stories. These comments by well-meaning adults, as well as our own observations of ourselves in certain situations, contributed to how we see ourselves today, and how capable we think we are.

For most people, the idea of being a published author is way beyond their current identity, so we literally have to change our identity in order to achieve this goal or we will sabotage ourselves and get in our own way.

We have to get clear on what we want and we have to consider what it will take for us to be a successful, published author, and then we have to open our minds to the possibilities of becoming that person.

What does a successful author say? What do they do? How do they speak? How did they behave? How do they talk about themselves? How do they present themselves? How do they show up in life? How did they use their time and resources? And how do other people see them?

Now you have to consider: what would you have to do in order to get comfortable with that vision of yourself? It's really just another version of yourself, but if you can't get comfortable with it you won't allow it to come into your reality.

Using visualisation is a really powerful tool that will help you to get comfortable with a new way of being and doing things – a new identity.

A year ago, I was planning a trip to Japan with my family and I decided I wanted to lose some weight before I went. I knew we would be doing a lot of walking and I didn't want to be tired or slow the family down. I was also thinking about the fact that Japanese people are a small race, so knowing I would be comfortable in plane, train and bus seats was important.

I started using a visualisation for weight loss by Jon Gabriel and continued using it consistently for 4 months.

During my visualisations I saw myself on the scales holding my plane ticket which clearly stated my name, destination: Japan, and the date. Beneath the ticket I visualised the scales and I saw a weight that I thought would be a comfortable weight to be at when we travelled.

I tried a few different things during that four months but nothing really shifted. Then, something happened with my health that demanded my full attention and helped me to make the decision to change my diet.

I was so busy that I forgot about the visualisations, but an interesting thing happened just 2 days before we left for Japan. I jumped on the scales and, to my delight, I was within 300g of the weight I had seen every night for 4 months in my visualisation.

Further to that, however, It is months since I returned, and even though I stayed on much the same diet with the same amount of activity that saw my weight drop, my weight has stopped at the weight I saw in my visualisation. That is how powerful practicing visualisation can be.

The moral of the story: if you can't see yourself as an author, you won't become one.

Plan the Work, Then Work the Plan

The third step in writing your book and getting it published is to plan the work, then work the plan.

There are a lot of steps involved in writing and publishing a book, and as I said earlier, writing is a small part of the big picture. It is certainly a smaller part than people realise, so let me go through what some of those steps are and what you need to do to complete them successfully.

(i) The first thing is to plan your book.
What do you want to write about?
Who do you want to write to/for?
What are their problems/concerns and how are you going to help them solve them?

Knowing the answers to these questions is very important because this gives you the outline for what you're going to create, and it will be like your lighthouse and keep you on track with your writing.

(ii) The next thing is to work out a writing schedule.

If you have a planner and you started from the end with your launch date, you would then work backwards in the timeline to a place where we can easily calculate how much time you have to write.

From there, you would calculate how many words you need to write on a daily or weekly basis.

How many words do you want to write in total?
How many words do you want to complete each week?
What days and times can you dedicate to your writing?
What is possible for you?
How many words do you plan to write each session knowing what you limitations are?

It is really important to note here that if you set intentions to do something that you physically, mentally or emotionally cannot complete, you will be setting yourself up for failure, so be honest with yourself about what you can and can't do.

(iii) The next thing is to create what I like to call a *sacred writing space* where you feel inspired and where you can you work undisturbed.

Inspiration is so important. What can you add to your writing space that will help you focus and work efficiently?

I have a few different spaces that I can work well in and I'm very aware of the things that inspire me. When you become aware of what works for you, it will help you to get to your goal faster.

For me, listening to music without words gets me into a great flow. Being near the waterfront and having tea and snacks at hand really help so that I don't have to get up and move about too often. I choose times when I won't be disturbed and block out time for writing in the calendar. Otherwise things happen, phones ring, Facebook pings and people come along, and before you know it, your time has been eaten up with things that don't bring you closer to your goal of writing a book.

Protect your writing time and space.

(iv) The next step is to complete your first draft.

Having worked out a completion date for your first draft, you will want to keep regular check along the way that you are, in fact, on track to finishing your first draft on time, otherwise you will have to adjust other things in the schedule and it may even impact on your launch date.

(v) The next thing to do is to format your book for print.

You need to decide which platform you will use for printing, and then you need to find out what they're formatting specs are. You also need to think about what you like in a book and how you want your book to look and feel to your reader.

Formatting specs includes things like page size, font style, font size, heading style and size, whether you have your headings hyper-linked to a table of contents, line spacing, whether you use justification, etc.

You don't only need to meet the needs of the Print-On-Demand (POD) Platform or Printer before you can upload and publish your book – your formatting also needs to be consistent throughout the book to give it a professional look and feel and to make it a pleasant experience for your reader.

(vi) Once the first draft is complete, you will want to make sure your cover design is finalised. It is best to do this here before it goes to the editor, because the editor will likely also edit the cover.

However, I really like the idea of creating an electronic 3D version of your book cover before you start writing, because it is very inspiring to see your book. It helps to make it feel real and it helps you to write.

Something else to consider at this point is that if you are writing non-fiction, put your face front and centre on the book cover. It is a powerful affirmation and a powerful way to show up for yourself and your reader.

You may change the look of your book cover or you may change your title or wording on the cover before you go to print, but it's still a worthwhile exercise to create the cover early and use the visualisation of what your book *might* look like to inspire you to write.

Some things to consider while creating your book cover are what sort of a look and feel do you want to have, what message or information do you want to get across? Will you design something for yourself, or will you get someone to design your cover for you?

(vii) The next thing you need to do is to engage a professional editor.

Happily, if you don't already know a professional editor, there are lots of them on the planet who are really excited at the prospect of editing your book, so you won't have to look far, and certainly at MJL Publications we have editors on hand waiting to help you create the best possible version of your story.

Once the first draft edit is complete, you will need to go through and choose which recommendations you will or will not adopt. This is entirely up to you. It is after all, your book, your work of art and your creation, so you get the final say.

Unless, of course, you are going through a traditional publisher. They might not allow you to have the final say.

(viii) Now it's time to seek testimonials for your book. Three or four would be great.

Who do you know who would read your book and give you a testimonial? Who would you *like* to receive a testimonial from? Is there a particular professional or a celebrity that you would like to have read your work and endorse it? Who would your readers respect and listen to?

Whoever you have in mind, ask them. They may say no, but they may say yes. You never know until you ask.

You might also want a celebrity or professional to write a forward for your book. Once again, ask, and you may just get what you want.

Once you have your testimonials you can insert them into your manuscript, and you can start formatting your manuscript for eBooks.

(ix) Format your manuscript for eBooks.

It is important to create as many formats of your book as possible. We all take information in in different ways. I personally prefer Audible, because as I get older I want to go to sleep as soon as I start reading, so I find listening to books very efficient and I can be doing other things at the same time, like washing, cooking or walking.

If I really like a book I will also buy the eBook version, because I like carrying books with me on my devices and having options all the time. With Apple devices and some Androids, you have accessibility via text to speech, so I can still listen to an eBook.

And, if I really like a book, I will also buy the print copy.

There are three popular platforms for eBooks that I format for at MJL Publications. They are PDF, of course, which can be read on any device. Then there is .mobi, which is the Kindle format for Amazon, and then there is e.pub, which is for just about every other device such as Barnes and Noble, Nook, Google and iBooks.

My experience at MJL Publications has taught me that print books are still by far the most popular form for a book.

(x) So, now that you have formatted your eBooks, you can start planning your launch.

It's time to think about when and where you will have your book launch. Who do you want to invite and share that moment with? Would like to make it a fundraiser? Will there be catering? Will there be entertainment? Would you do all the work? Or will you get someone to do it for you?

The more time you give yourself to plan this event the better. This will ensure that it is a great and memorable occasion shared with as many people as you want in the manner that you want.

This is your time to shine, so plan it well.

(xi) By now, you should have received your testimonials and inserted them into your manuscript, so it's time to forward the manuscript to the Printer you chose, or to upload it to the POD platform that you chose.

That platform might be Lulu, CreateSpace or Ingram Spark.

At MJL we use Lulu for a variety of reasons to do with geography, formatting and pricing, but whichever platform you chose you will now need to upload your document so that you can order a proof copy.

Once the proof copy is on the way, you can officially launch your presales. That means finding a way to let your friends, family, clients and followers know that your book is for sale and will be available in the very near future.

You want to make it as easy as possible for them all to buy your book from you and pay you without you being in their presence, so that means some sort of webpage: a Facebook page or some sort of electronic platform where your followers along with your friends, family and clients can go to order and pay for your book.

The next steps will be dependent, of course, on whether or not you're happy with your proof copy. If you still need to make some changes it's easy to do with print on demand, so make your changes and upload your adjusted manuscript.

(xii) You will want to start promoting your book launch now.

Where and how can you promote it? Would it be by invitation or will it be open to the public? Do you want to attract media attention? Which papers, magazines, radio stations or news outlets might be interested in your story? Have you given them plenty of time to cover the event?

(xiii) You will want to order final copies now for the launch.

Hopefully, you will have sold lots of copies in the pre-sales launch and you can order them now so that they are ready for those people to collect at the launch or to be posted to them. You will also want additional copies to sell at the launch.

(xiv) Now it's time for the book launch. Hooray! The Day Has Come!

Are you relaxed? Do you feel good? Are you happy with your hair, your outfit, your speech, and the launch program? What do you hope to achieve today?

(xv) And finally, it's time to plan your marketing and put your plan into action. You may want to engage a marketing specialist or a media specialist to help you to plan your marketing strategies.

How are you going to continually market your book so that sales grow and demand for you and your services are constantly increasing?

Marketing is an ongoing part of the business of being a published author.

I trust that you now have a much better picture of what is involved in writing and publishing your book. It seems bigger and more complicated than what it actually is, but like everything else in life, there is a way to do things. We just need to find out what that way is, follow the steps and get help when we need it.

I have a number of free resources at my website at to help you get started, to identify where you need help and to keep you on track, including:

1. a free Writing and Publishing Checklist,
2. a free Writing and Publishing Planner,
3. a free Visualisation to help with identity,
4. a free meditation to help authors create flow in their writing, and
5. 2 free book templates.

Find these at
http://www.mjlpublications.com.au/freeresources.

When you are filling out your planner I encourage you to start with your launch date and work backwards to ensure that you have plenty of time for each of the tasks that need to be taken care of.

You may be excited and want to make things happen in less than 12 months, but when you have a tight schedule, things often happen that get in the way, so don't disappoint yourself by not allowing enough time for everything.

If you are seriously considering writing a book in the next twelve months I encourage you to join me – and lots of other authors – in my *Write A Book Club* over at MJL Publications. As a member of the club you will have access to a range of products and services that will help you get your book written and published over the course of the next 12 months.

Those products and services include:

1: A Book Planning and Scheduling Session.

This is such an exciting session, because this is where we create your ***personal blueprint for your book*** including a ***12-month step-by-step plan*** of what needs to be done and when it needs to be done by.

We will take you through a specific process that will help you to refine what your core message is, who your target audience is, how best to articulate your message for that particular audience and what type of support you will need to complete your book.

Then we put all of that information – every step and every chore – onto your very own 12-month plan so that you can see exactly what needs to be done and when it needs to be done.

At the end of this session you will have your step-by-step plan and you'll be able to get into action straight away. And, you'll be really excited about publishing your book. This is when it starts to feel real and you know it's not just *going* to happen, it's *actually* happening.

2: Twelve months access to Author Gym

Author Gym is a fantastic subscription-based membership which gives authors access to ***unlimited laser coaching sessions*** over the course of their 12-month membership.

These 15-minute sessions can be used for coaching in writing or in publishing and will depend on where the author is at and what they need in order to complete their book.

3:    Twelve months access to Group Coaching

With Group Coaching you will have access to **weekly live coaching sessions** where we help our authors to be the best they can be and get the most they can out of their writing and publishing experience.

This is a fantastic way to **build on your writing and publishing skills** and **address any concerns or questions you have** around your own experience. It's also a great way to mix with and learn from the other authors in *the Club*.

4:    Access to twelve online Masterclasses

Our masterclasses include topics such as Writing To Engage, Formatting Your Book, Publishing for Beginners, Copyright and Trademarking, The Business of Writing, Education Based Marketing, Leveraging your Book, Book Marketing, Building Your Author Platform and much, *much* more.

5:    Access to a private community on Facebook where you can socialise, interact and push through barriers with like-minded people.

6:    And finally, Club members will have their book formatted for the three most popular eBook platforms at the end of the twelve months.

You can find out everything you need to know about the Write A Book Club at
http://www.mjlpublications.com.au/jointheclub.

To end my chapter, I would like to leave you with this thought:

Don't get it right. Get it written.

Deborah Fay specialises in helping Small Business Owners to become the *author*-ity in their field of work, to completely set themselves apart from their competition and to reach more of their target market with greater ease. She does this by helping them to package their knowledge and expertise into a book, which they can use as a tool to help their clients get to know, like and trust them, and ultimately buy from them.

Deborah Fay is an author, publisher and self-publishing coach with a background in counselling. As the founder and principal of MJL Publications she has helped more than 40 aspiring authors to share their stories and make a real difference in the world.

Are you ready to consider publishing as a means to making a difference?

Go to MJL Publications at
http://www.mjlpublications.com.au/freeresources/
for your free book templates, free writing and publishing checklist, your free 12-month planner and your free visualisation.

Pat Armitstead
ANTIZAC

How refusing
Prozac changed
my llife

We have medicalised unhappiness and are in danger of losing sight of our souls. ANTIZAC is soul awakening and I will prescribe freely. Dr Robin Kelly, Author The Human Hologram

Writing is a Huge Part of Being Fully Self-Expressed

by Pat Armitstead

You know that saying, "The writings on the wall"? Well, my first sojourn into the world of the written word was actually at the age of 18 months when I "wrote" on the wall beside my cot with the contents of my nappy. Yes... I was supposed to be sleeping, but creative expression was kicking in already!

Fast forward to my years of nursing and I documented many factual progress reports. Not particularly inspiring, but there began my real foundations for expression. I had always wanted to be an artist, but my mother told me to get a real job, and so it was I went with nursing.

(Just quietly, if you are a nurse or a doctor, there is no room for creative expression!)

It was another 16 years before I got into the creative zone again when I started my own video production company. I studied journalism and scriptwriting, wrote ads, interviewed for the news, 20:20 and 60 Minutes, and created 10 documentaries of my own. One of those became a best seller, selling 5000 copies in 12 weeks. By putting my words on the page and having a colleague create a jingle, I also sold a shared TV advertising package to over 300 businesses and generated $400,000 cash flow. Words became very important to me.

I placed ads in specialty magazines and sold products, mostly videos in that fashion and from my studio shop front. I wrote speeches and gave talks on advertising and marketing. I didn't know it at the time, but this was all fodder for my future foray into writing, or as we say, authoring!

A series of losses at the turn of the century and I landed on the shores of New Zealand. I committed that if I was going to not just survive, but thrive, I would have to get clever. So, I secured Mike Hutcheson, then MD of Saatchi and Saatchi Auckland, as my mentor! Then, I committed that I would be published every month as part of my outreach. There is a trail on Google that shows some of that pathway, with me being published in newspapers, on TV and radio, and writing columns. A shameless self-promoter, I even ran programs showing others how to do this.

The big writing breakthrough came when I secured a column with the NZ *Business to Business* newspaper writing a weekly column called 'Humour Works'. I had this column for many years. In a publication full of serious news, the column stood out and got a lot of attention, not just in New Zealand, but globally as well. The most popular was a column called 'I flirt, therefore I sell'. Controversial much? Apparently, it was inappropriate to even contemplate the idea that one might be flirtatious.

That led to being invited to present to a singles group presenting 'I flirt therefore I date!'. And that led to a 12-month public program series called 'Overcoming Flirtophobia'. I wrote a booklet on that. Insert cheeky smile here!

I was invited not long after that to be interviewed for a book called *Woman 2 Woman – NZ Women Share Their Experiences of Career and Business*. My interview was around the value of having a mentor in business. Published in 2003, this positioned me alongside some of the most successful women in the country and gave credence to my work, which was pretty revolutionary for its time. My business is called Joyology. When I reviewed that inclusion, much of what the journalist wrote is actually not quite true. Seeing this mis-representation has heightened my resolve to position myself and others factually and in the fullness of who they really are.

My first book was called *Humour Works* and was fashioned after the column I had in the newspaper. Funnily enough (pun intended), a man I had been dating asked for 5 weeks off from the relationship, and in the interim I was invited to speak at Australia's first Humour, Engagement and Wellbeing Conference. I did not have a book and resolved that I would have one completed in the 6 weeks before the conference. I took the best of the columns and rewrote them so they suited being published in a book. I asked the winners of my Humour in Business Awards if they would sponsor the first 100 copies, and they agreed. So, *New Zealand Window Shades* have a full page at the front of this book and have been promoted widely as a result. This has sold well over 5000 copies, a best seller in New Zealand! This book was self-published, and I sold most copies when I was at speaking events.

I already knew about and had sent many press releases, but now I set myself a task to become very polished at this. Interestingly, it was picked up by a media commentator John Bishop, who wrote, *"Pat commits the cardinal management sin of spreading joy and making people smile. If her practices become widely adopted, going to work will become fun and people will enjoy the experience. Ultimately, she is a dangerous subversive to dullness, mediocrity and boredom. Why can't we have more like her?"*

The first presentation I gave in NZ following its release was to a group of doctors, and one fed back in his closing remarks, *"Pat Armitstead is New Zealand's answer to Patch Adams"*. Patch Adams himself wrote on receiving a draft copy, *"Just returned from around the world to find your lovely words and wandering contract with the worlds happy people ... look forward to playing with you in Russia again!"*

Oh, yes, and my man did come back, but his first comment when he caught up with my news about being published was that I was "nothing but an over-achiever". He was correct, of course, but the relationship ended in that conversation!

In 2006, a man called Chris Dodds had found the silver lining in his own life events and brought together some remarkable business people in New Zealand, including myself, to share stories of inspiration for New Zealand high school students. This country has a very high rate of domestic violence, poverty and youth suicide. A book called *Silver linings on the long white cloud* was produced, and copies given to every high school in New Zealand. It was also placed in every library. Chris funded this from his own money.

Creating this kind of series is a wonderful legacy.

This book and my other book, *Humour Works*, were found in Greymouth library by the Police Chaplain in the few days following the Greymouth Pike River Mine disaster where 26 men lost their lives in an explosion. The chaplain rang me saying, *"I have just read your book. This disaster has really shaken this whole community to its core. I went in search of something new, as all my previous learnings were not enough to manage the shock and grief of this event"*. You see, we don't know where things will go and the effect they will have.

My next book, *ANTIZAC – A joyful prescription for the unhappiness epidemic*, was actually born on my tour with Patch Adams in 2004, but not published till 2012. It encompassed a philosophy I shared every time I spoke to people moving through tough times, which was to be creating their own prescription. I wrote this "prescription" for myself as I surfaced from those losses but did not articulate it in great detail, till 2012.

A – amuse …
N – nthuse …
T – trust …
I – intuition …
Z – zeal …
A – attitude …
C – creativity …

There are 7 chapters each under these headings, and I made the first introductory page for each chapter distinctive in its layout. The first chapter is called, "Once upon a not so amusing time", and there follows a dictionary meaning of the word "amuse". The other chapters are of similar vein. At 120 pages, it is a small book, and each chapter can be read in isolation. There are activities or thought-leading questions at the close of each chapter.

At this time, I was finding more flow in my writing and I attracted wonderful endorsements from business leaders, medical colleagues, and international speaking peers before it was even complete! **Robyn Stent**, former Health and Disability Commissioner New Zealand, wrote: *"Pat is one of the most positive, energetic people I have ever met. Pat's approach is always focused on the particular environment in which she is speaking, training or entertaining. It's high time we focussed on proactive prevention of health problems and stress."*

Dr Robin Kelly, NZ author of the award winning *The Human Hologram – Living Your Life in Harmony with the Unified Field*, wrote the forward for me. Having people who hold esteemed positions endorse our products is priceless, and the testimonials received can be used anywhere in promotions.

Generating this kind of response, endorsement wise, requires a lot of time in the planning process, deciding who your book is for and who will be served. I built those relationships along the way, and it was then so much easier to be making the request as times got closer. Fortune favours those who dare, and so I dared to approach many wise people for support and guidance. I have a friend who calls himself "the Maverick", and his first book was written with the 2nd half upside down. So, essentially, you could read it from the front or the back.

Humour sells!

Having a peer group who support your authoring endeavours is so valuable. Not so much that they become your editors, but more to help you hold your space and your commitment so that you can complete on the project. Authoring and speaking masterminds were a big part of this journey for me, aligning with those who had gone before me and had wisdom and experience to share. Bill Potter, "The Maverick", was a genius, and I loved having his quirky world view as a reminder of wonderful individual expression!

The Inspiration Bible is the most recent print book I have featured in. 365 authors contributed one page each for the most amazing collection of inspirational stories. Contributing to this kind of book takes a different discipline, requiring you to be succinct. Each person contributed a fairly small sum which gave the producer an ample amount to develop an amazing book. For each copy that is sold, one is given away, fostering so much goodwill as it wings its way to those who need to hear these stories. I had numerous re-writes to capture the essence of my story without losing the meaning behind it. A gala event was held in Melbourne to celebrate the launch, adding pomp and ceremony to a significant publication. Dr John Demartini was at the launch as a featured guest, supporting Emily Gower, the creator.

I am currently writing my own story, the draft titled *Joyful Empowerment – The Only Way Out is Through*. I began about four years ago, but ill health intervened and then old wounds surfaced that needed to be healed before I could invest myself fully into the writing. I believe we find our intuitive self when we have healed the past and can experience more flow. We are probably never done with this process but do reach a point where we can sit and articulate what needs to go on the page.

At the Get Known Be Seen Author Expo in 2018, I crafted a collar that looked like an artist's palette, using my book covers and coloured pencils. I wanted to inspire potential authors to show their true colours... indeed, to sharpen their pencils. I painted my face as I stepped through my presentation, the idea being to bring colour and art to life on the face of my life. I wanted to share in that window of time how sequential hand movements, like those used in handwriting, activate large regions of the **brain** responsible for thinking, language, healing and working memory. Every book I have written starts with me handwriting, and then I move on to the computer once I have my thoughts down. I experience more flow in handwriting, and I think there is something about body/mind connection with the pen and paper.

When we are clear on our vision and purpose, when we have our intellectual property sorted, it creates clarity and direction for us. My vision is to show people how to find joy when it appears there is none. My mission is to be a voice for all that is joyful about humanity. I am here to foster full self-expression – that's my own and others'.

I was a registered nurse with a major in education, plus I am a master practitioner of Neurolinguistics and a certified mBIT coach. A professional speaker and motivator, I am an authority on leadership, communication, grief and stress. Over the past 20 years, I have given highly educational and entertaining presentations into both the business and health sectors on topics such as mental health in the workplace; stress, humour and health; authentic leadership, self-expression and productivity; and storytelling and engagement in the workplace.

I call myself a pioneer and thought-leader in the area of joy; as a transformational agent, I have championed the human spirit leading people to find joy and have devoted my life to helping others to transform their lives. It is my unique personal perspectives, traumatic past, repeated losses and eventual mastery as a multi award-winning speaker, TV and radio host and exhibiting artist that enable me to fill this place. I love storytelling and combine positive psychology principles, emotional intelligence and neuroscience with real human experiences to bring understanding and meaning to life events.

I see crisis as a catalyst for personal growth and ongoing transformation, enabling high levels of intimate communication and authentic expression. **One of my favourite sayings is, "You can't lift your bottom line if people are down."** 1:5 people are medicated for depression, costing us up to 200 billion per year, and in Australia alone there are 3000 suicides per year. That's 8 people every day!

Joy makes a difference!

I have toured internationally with Patch Adams and shared the stage live and online with speaking greats such as Jack Canfield, Bruce Lipton, John Demartini and Patricia Fripp.

Since 2001, I have delivered over 600 keynotes at conferences, and worked in-house with leaders and their teams developing high trust environments, building resilience and lifting morale. I have been able to bring this message to more than a million people in 20+ countries through presentations, media appearances and my own radio program which was honoured by the Auckland Mayor with a civic reception.

"Across the globe, many people lack joy, harmony, and trust, and are prone to doubt. They have become despondent and depressed, fail to be their word, sit in overwhelm; others are

resigned and intolerant. Others show cynicism and act confused, and many lack confidence, all of which results in emotional flatlining, lack of engagement, poor productivity and, more recently, unresolved grief, poor mental health and suicides." **I work with individuals to help them transition through tough times.**

I am creative, and I am an ideas person. For aspiring authors, I run a program developing speaking, authoring and going to market, and this triple combination has proven invaluable for those stepping up to be more confident in all 3 areas. Readers are invited to take advantage of a complimentary discovery session.

The World's First Joyologist
Multi Award-Winning Speaker, Facilitator, Author
Past President of the National Speakers Association NZ
Speaker of the Year 2002 NSANZ

0487 105 785 | pat@joyology.co.nz | Skype: Joyologist

www.joyology.co.nz

EXCLUSIVE OFFER FROM PAT ARMITSTEAD
For the
Get Known Be Seen Expo

As an exclusive offer to participants in The Get Known Be Seen Expo, Pat is offering the following:

- You can all have a free copy of my e-book *A Way With Words*, which shows how to use written and spoken words to inspire and engage your audience

- Join my Unleashing Brilliance FB closed group – currently free membership:
https://www.facebook.com/groups/220091198726920

- 20% off my Transformational Speaker Program. A free Discovery session is a prelude to this:
http://www.joyology.co.nz/transformational-speaker-centre.html

From Coward to Legal Lioness
by Cathryn Warburton

When tragedy struck, I was just six years old. My three year old friend disappeared. As the search for Mishak dwindled, I could not understand why everyone was not still out looking for him. Nor could I understand why they called it a search "party", when it was an unimaginable nightmare.

The sound of Mishack's mother wailing like a wounded animal, the smell of the dry African dirt, the confusion and the terror of it all remain with me to this day. So many times in the days, weeks and even decades that followed, I wondered if anybody could have done anything to have prevented the tragedy.

More importantly, I wondered if there was anything I could have done, or should have done, that might have made him more aware of stranger danger.

Where was he? Was he cold? Was he lonely? Surely he must be scared? Did he think no one was looking for him? What was he eating?

The questions were endless. And there were no answers. As day turned into weeks, then months, then years. Still no answers. Only questions echoing in my mind.

That nightmare shaped me into the protector that I would later become.

I chose a legal career, because I felt it was a way that I could not only honour my lost friend, but also make a real difference to those who needed help.

Unfortunately, Mishack was never found, although a core group of family and friends continued to search for him year after year. Eventually even the police had to admit that he was likely dead. They said that there had been a spate of young boys kidnapped in the area and their best theory was that they were murdered and their body parts used for black medicine rituals (a detail that still makes me ill to this day, and certainly one that I should never have overheard as a small child imagining what had befallen her friend).

After the nightmare of my friend disappearing, I became hypervigilant, watching out for danger on behalf of others. It made sense for me to go into a career where I would be trained to help others avoid potential disaster. I find it particularly fulfilling when I can help people before they get into legal trouble. This is why I put so much effort and time into creating free online videos to help business owners keep out of legal hot water. Friend me on Facebook to get access to these videos – https://www.facebook.com/LegalLioness

I am now known as the "The Legal Lioness". I am the recipient of multiple international business awards.

I have a passion for protecting businesses from business bullies and bringing business communities together. I would love you to share about your business on my business Facebook group:

https://www.facebook.com/groups/BizBoosters/

Interestingly, I grew up quite a timid and scared person. I was terrified of public speaking, which I attributed to being kicked out of the choir when I was just six years old. I had been practising faithfully with the choir for the entire year for the end of year Christmas pageant. The school had been divided into two groups. A small group was in the choir, and the larger group was acting in the pageant. Two weeks before the Christmas pageant the choir Mistress decided that something did not sound right with the choir, and she made each person sing individually in front of the whole group. Every single other person was given high praise, until it came to me.

Then she told me, in front of everybody, how dreadful I sounded and our how I was ruining the sound of the choir. From that moment, and for many decades afterwards, I was convinced that every sound and every word that came out of my mouth was rubbish and worthless. I wish I could find that choir Mistress today, and let her know the damage that she caused.

So, having being kicked out of the choir so unceremoniously, I was devastated, not only by the personal insult relating to how I was ruining the sound of the choir, but also because I desperately wanted to be in the Christmas pageant with every other child in the school. She told me I could ask the other teacher if I could be a sheep or a rock in the other part of the pageant.

When I asked the other teacher if I could participate in some way in the pageant, I was told no I could not. Only people who had come to rehearsals with the rest of the group were entitled to be in the pageant.

Of course, it was monumentally unfair, I had been to every choir rehearsal, and then been told I was not good enough just weeks before the event. Choir rehearsals and pageant rehearsals were on at the same time, so there is no way I could physically have gone to the pageant rehearsals as I was at choir rehearsals.

Well, you can imagine how crushing it was for a six year old, desperately enthusiastic to be in the Christmas pageant, to be told that not only was she ruining the choir, but she was not even good enough to be a sheep or even a rock in the Christmas pageant.

I am not sure if I really had any self-esteem before that moment, but certainly from that moment forward, and for decades afterwards, any ounce of self-esteem that I might have had was crushed out of me.

For years, I never said a word in public, unless forced to.

Man! The year that I was six was one kick in the guts after another.

From Coward to Legal Lioness

This is why I have called my biography *From Coward To Legal Lioness*, because if I could go from wanting to drop out of law school when I heard that an oral examination was compulsory, to defending clients in front of three judges in the Court of Appeal, or appearing on radio or in front of live crowds of 200 people; anyone can overcome their fears to live their true authentic passionate lives.

Some days I can almost still not believe that I frequently speak at conferences, business groups, on radio and podcasts and that my 2-minute videos "busting legal myths" are becoming a social media sensation. I have secured intellectual property for international pop stars and television shows. I have personally argued intellectual property and contract disputes in court, and have over 1000 trade mark registrations under my belt.

So, what led me from being a timid and shy girl who was literally paralysed with fear at the thought of speaking publicly, to becoming the Legal Lioness?

At first, it was to honour my friend, Mishak, who had disappeared all those years ago. I still had within me a stubborn and burning determination to help other people, particularly those who might not even see the danger they may be in.

When my first son was born, I was working for a big law firm, which was one of the top law firms in the field of intellectual property. I was starting to feel restless, and wanted to be at home with my son, but they called me into work because my team leader was ill and they needed me to take over. One of the partners told me it was such a wonderful opportunity to be acting team leader, I should not expect to be paid for my time while doing it! He (of course) expected me to donate up to three months of my time to a profit-making firm for the "benefit" to me of the experience of being "acting team leader". I asked if I could have flexible hours because my son was so young and unwell, and I was stepping into the breach to help them. They said no. Flexible hours were out of the question.

I went home in tears, feeling dreadful. I was torn. I wanted to be with my son, he was so tiny and quite ill. And yet, the firm had been good to me, and I wanted to help out because my team leader was unable to be at work.

Then, my husband, who is an amazing inspiration to me, asked me the following question.

"Do you want to be a partner in a firm that treats their staff in the way that you have been treated?"

Of course the answer was a resounding NO! And then I started remembering why I had become a lawyer in the first place, to help people, not just to worry about billable hours, but to really make a difference.

The decision to resign and form my own firm, Acacia Law (www.acacialaw.com), took 20 minutes over dinner. Although in reality, in my heart, I knew that I needed to be the master of my own destiny, to truly be the type of lawyer that I wanted to be, and not be constrained by the large firm and their expectations which did not align with my heart.

Rocky Road

A year after starting my own law firm, my husband (Mark) quit his job and joined me in Acacia Law as a partner.

We specialise in business and intellectual property law, which is very close to Mark's heart. His grandfather was an amazing inventor, who invented special technology that changed the face of railway travel and is used in railways even to this day. Unfortunately, he was very trusting and not very business savvy, and had his invention stolen by his boss.

Mark's grandfather ended up estranged from his family, an alcoholic, who died a pauper on a park bench. His genius was not recognised by his family members, and they thought he was a failure. Worse than that, he believed he was useless, while someone else made millions off his own hard work.

This is one of the reasons why our work is so personal to Mark and me. Every person who creates intellectual property is reminiscent of Mark's grandfather, and we are on a personal mission to make sure that they reap the fruits of their labour as they deserve.

Certainly, running our own firm has not all been sunshine and roses.

Like any business, we have faced many challenges and have had to adapt as society changes and technology changes. When we started our business in 2003, I could never have imagined chatting with strangers on Facebook, much less making business connections there.

We started our business in New Zealand, and then the law changed and the government decided to amalgamate the patent and trademark attorney profession into the Australian profession. At the same time, international trade mark attorneys became allowed to file trademarks directly into Australia and New Zealand. These two facts dropped our income by about 60%, and we made the heartrending decision to move our family and business to Australia, leaving behind Mark's parents. Thankfully, my mum, who lived with us by that point, was able to come with us, and at the time of writing this, is 82 years old and enjoying her granny flat attached to our house in a Brisbane suburb.

We had to reinvent our business in a new location where we knew nobody, and we had to find a new client base in a competitive market.

More recently, law firms and patent and trademark attorney firms are turning to artificial intelligence, and spending millions of dollars replacing lawyers and attorneys with computer programs. Our industry is being taken over by robots, and if we do not show our value to our clients, they will simply go with the cheaper robotic alternative, because there is no way that we can offer to do things as cheaply as an automated lawyer can.

Some might think that this is the end for Acacia Law and The Legal Lioness.

They would be wrong.

This is not the most difficult thing we have gone through as a family or as a firm.

We have battled through both of our children having chronic illness. Both of them having autism. My husband suffering from such a severe sinus infection that it caused an infection on the brain and the specialist said that if he did not operate within the week, Mark would not live to see Christmas (which was only three weeks away at that time). We nursed my father through motor neurones disease until he took his last breath peacefully with the family holding his hands. There is a litany of other personal difficulties that I could share here, but I prefer not to. I prefer to focus on love and light and energy.

Did I want to lie down and give up at times? Of course, I did, for an hour or two. I let the sadness wash over me, and then I took a deep breath and got on with whatever needed to be done.

Robots taking over our industry?

That is nothing compared to the personal struggles we have been through.

All it means to me is another chance to reinvent how I help people, in a way that no robot could.

Is it difficult? Absolutely!

Is it scary, knowing that other small law firms are shutting up shop by the dozens? It certainly is.

But I do not let any of that paralyse me. I choose to take action. I choose to try new things, find new ways of offering the service that other small businesses out there need. Might some of my current client base prefer to deal with a robot who is cheaper than me? Yes, they will. But they were never my ideal clients to start with.

My ideal clients are the ones who are interested in me and my story, who want to know me as a person, who love the fact that to me they are more than just a client or a business. To me they are a piece of a larger puzzle. Each of us connected in a unique and special way.

I am finding new skills and learning new things about myself all the time. I have discovered that, contrary to what I would have thought, I am good at networking online. I have learned that there is a deep hunger for my legal knowledge. Posting two minute videos online, that really help small business owners avoid inadvertently infringing copyright, or getting into other legal disputes, are a way that I can connect with real business owners, who appreciate me and want to work with me. Having my books published, gives me credibility with them, when they do not yet know me, and helps them to engage with me more quickly, than they otherwise might have.

Not all of these online contacts turn into business, of course. Some only want the freebies. Even that is a bonus for me, because although they may not want to engage me as a lawyer, if they hear of someone who needs a lawyer, they will often refer that person to me.

Also, I am meeting more and more successful women who are so busy running their businesses, that they need somebody like me, someone who they can trust, someone who they know has gone through the hard times and been successful, and still continues to go through difficulties, and never gives up. They need a lawyer who truly has their back and actually gives a damn about them and their businesses.

These women do not want some faceless robot. They do not want one of the thousands of lawyers listed on the Internet who come across as more interested in billing and case files, than the person behind the business.

So how have I done it?

I have followed the energy in the direction of things that energise me, even if it terrifies me.

I knew that I needed to help people, and I knew that I needed to be in a profession where I could warn people before they got into trouble. Every time I have stepped off that path, I have been miserable. BUT I have to take care to temper that with a big dose of common sense. For example, if you are energised about being an actress, but nobody will give you acting roles, it is not a sensible choice for your life, and you may have to work at something else to earn money while you are getting your dream going. So as far as common sense goes, there are two elements that are important:

1. can you make a living from following your passion? And if not, how will you support yourself while you follow your passion? and
2. make sure that while you are following your passion you are not infringing somebody else's intellectual property or allowing somebody else to take advantage of your intellectual property?

If you are feeling exhausted and worn out, as all small business owners feel from time to time, take time to centre yourself, however that looks for you, whether that is getting into nature, being with people you love, or accessing a coach or mentor. Think about which path energises you, and which path saps the life out of you. Running your own business will be difficult and will take a lot of energy, but if you're following your passion, you should get a buzz from it. If you have lost the buzz, take time to rediscover it, or you will end up burnt out and unhappy.

Following your dream and passion without having the correct legal protections in place to start with, is only going to end in tears. Recently, I had a new client who told me that when he was 10 years old he created business cards for himself, with a particular brand name that he had created. Now he's in his 40s, and due to an accident cannot follow his chosen career, and has decided to start his own business with his dream brand that he thought up as a child. He spent $10,000 on design and promotional material before coming to me for legal advice. I checked the trademarks register and discovered that his "dream brand" likely infringes a trade mark registered quite recently. If he had started with brand protection, he would have saved a lot of money and heart-ache. Now he faces having to select a different brand, and he is devastated.

Of course, I am there to help him as best I can in the circumstances, but my goal is to help business owners understand that getting the legalities and intellectual property issues in their business right at the start, can be a very wise investment in their dream business.

---------------------------------xxx---------------------------------

About me

I have written several books. Some relate to my life experiences, such as *From Coward to Legal Lioness*, where I explain my journey from being paralysed with fear at talking in public, to being a professional speaker. I hope that story will encourage others to follow their dreams. That book has been really great to reveal to people the person behind the image of the Legal Lioness, and to let people know that I am an ordinary person, who has had to overcome personal struggles, just like everyone else.

I am also just about to publish a book about living with family members suffering from chronic illness (and how to keep sane, thrive and run a business at the same time), and another about parenting a daughter with ASD.

My other books are quick easy guides about "legal essentials" (*Lawyer in Your Corner*) and "intellectual property essentials" (*What is Intellectual Property?*), for small business owners, to help keep them out of legal hot water. These books raise my profile and position me as an expert in the field, and are also a handy tool when I advise clients (they often want to read more after our consultation).

My name is Cathryn Warburton, and my clients call me The Legal Lioness. I am a lawyer and trade mark attorney with over 1000 trade mark registrations under my belt. I can help you with intellectual property protection world-wide.

My ideal client is a business owner who wants to protect their most valuable asset, their intellectual property. Some people think it will be too expensive to protect their intellectual property, which is why I offer free and low-cost online courses, so that even those on a budget can access this information. I even created an "assisted trade mark filing" program in which I walk you step-by step through the trade marking process.

Find out more at:

www.acacialaw.com or www.legallioness.com

I wrote my legal and intellectual property books because I saw new clients coming into my office making the same mistakes as others had over the years and I wanted a way to show people how to avoid costly and stressful legal mistakes.

My other books about my personal experiences growing up and dealing with chronic illness and ASD, have bubbled up out of me. I think that if my painful experience can teach just one other person one thing that helps them having to go through what I did (learning the hard way how to cope), then my suffering would be worth it.

My tip for aspiring authors

Whatever your story is, there is someone out there who needs to hear it. Don't keep it to yourself. If you write a little every week, your book will soon be finished.

Don't fuss too much over formatting and editing, you can always pay someone to help you with that.

If you are not a great "writer" then do what I do sometimes, I simply talk my words into my computer and convert it to text automatically. There are a lot of free programs that can do that for you, or you can use something like "Dragon Dictate", which is less costly than paying someone to transcribe for you. For me, "Dragon Dictate Professional" works very well. I love seeing my words pop onto the page as I speak them out loud.

If you are unsure if you are on the right track with your writing, join an online writing group. There are many that offer mutual feedback. Or find people who will read your drafts and provide you with honest feedback.

Writing does not have to be an individual pursuit. Nor do you have to pay top dollar to get people to help you. Whatever level you are at, you will be able to find people in your online networks who can help with editing etc. If you do not have an online network that can help, then spend a bit of time finding a group you can slot into (there are plenty of writing groups on Facebook, as just one example).

All the very best with your writing journey!

If you want to access my free legal and intellectual property tips for authors, please email me at tips@acacialaw.com and request a link to one of my free courses. You can use that same email address if you want to work directly with me to protect your legal or intellectual property rights in your book or business. I would love to hear from you.

Author, Lawyer, Speaker, Patent & TM attorney

Compelling story-teller.
Multi-international award-winning lawyer, trade mark attorney, patent attorney, author, speaker, radio interviewee, sought-after guest-blogger, mentor, entrepreneur, and mother-of-two.

Trans-Tasman (Au & NZ) Patent Attorney
& Australian Trade Mark Attorney (Partner)
QLD Solicitor (Director, Acacia Legal Pty Ltd)*

cathryn@acacialaw.com
www.acacialaw.com
Tel: +61 7 3418 0974
Fax: +61 7 3014 8765

Cathryn's clients love that her books cover the legal and IP essentials for small business. Cathryn was approached by a major publisher that wanted to re-publish her book *Lawyer in Your Corner* which explains legal essentials for small business in an easy to understand way.

Ask her why she said "no thanks" to that offer.

I Am Ria Sarah
by Ria Sarah

I am Ria Sarah. I have contemplated on how I would introduce myself, and the more I sat with it, the more I know that this is who I am. Nothing more, and nothing less. I am many things, and I am capable of so much. Recently, I have brought myself to ground zero and realised that 'I' am absolutely enough, and throughout this process I have realised the importance of Life and what you love and how important it is to each individual.

My business is Ria Sarah and consists of counselling and coaching.

My services include Counselling with Solution Focused Therapy and Cognitive Behaviour Therapy, as my expertise is in assisting you to find your place in the world and assist you to see the world in all its beauty.

Are you struggling through life?

Feel like you are at a crossroads in your life?

Feeling misunderstood?

You see, I know these feelings only too well; I too have been at a crossroads.

I have my own unique way of assisting those I work with.

Those people are the ones that know that 'something needs to change', and that's when we can work the magic.

Originally, I had been writing my own memoir/my story. As I wrote this, the life changing event of my mother going missing and being found transpired. As I wrote my own story, this book began to shape in my mind. As I considered writing about this experience, the memory of myself leaving my family home came to mind, and I realised how life had come full circle, with my mum leaving and when I did many *many* years ago.

You see, when I was 15, my mum's heart broke as I moved interstate to live with my father. I had no idea how much this affected my mother until months following her own disappearance.

It all came crashing down the night I got a call from my sister that my mum was missing, in April 2015.

Day after day went by and still no sign of her. As much as this felt like it shattered my soul into a million pieces, I will be forever grateful for my deep soul-searching in Feb 2014 because no matter how lost, distraught, alone that I felt at this time, there was something inside of me that just kept me going. At the time I couldn't quite explain it as everything was so emotional. Everywhere I turned I heard, "Have they found her?", "Any news on her mum?" …

My thoughts were, 'I can hear you.'

Those four days felt like an eternity and for me, and an experience I would never wish on anyone.

Looking back, I felt this space of peace within. The peace to carry on, to hold on to all that is dear, to be with what is.

This peace that I found within was and has been my saving grace.

As I talked about the event and started to plan and think about the book, I discovered that I had two parts already written.

The second part of the book was about my despair, my grief, and showing my mum how Australia came together in search of her being found safe and alive.

I knew there was a third part tying it all together.

As I gave the book space, it developed, and I also grew.

I stopped my own life story that I was writing early in 2018 with this knowing that I had to get this book written. So, that's when this book started being pieced together.

And as I did, I was also working on myself personally, doing some more learning, and it occurred to me that I had placed expectations on my mum.

I saw her, I see her in all her power. However, I quickly learnt that anyone and everyone is so much more than my expectations.

That's where my third part of the book came to life, and the inspiration for the title: *I love you, I'm Sorry.*

That's where I was Sorry.

As I complied this book and learnt so much about myself, I learnt unconditional love to it's core, I learnt about boundaries, and I have learnt about compassion for one's journey.

I let go of the expectations that existed in my mind, as I know that another person's greatness is so much more than a picture that I hold in my mind.

Writing this book, I had the desire for it to be a letter of love, a present for my mother.

When all said and done, it was so much more.

It was a journey; it was my journey. It was only ever my version of events, my story.

You see, it was not received in the way that I thought it was going to. This upset me greatly. However, the expectations I had of this book quickly dissipated and fell into thin air as the real and true reasons for this journey showed its true colours.

The real reason is: Me. The real truth is that I wrote this book about my journey, about how something so tragic changed my life. Not just with the writing, but with the outcome as well.

Writing my books came with its own set of massive learnings. I originally started writing to enter a competition to win a publishing contract, then I ventured into finding a book coach to assist me in getting the job done. Keep in mind that this is just my experience and not everyone's journey, and nor am I tarnishing anyone. However, for me, this journey with a coach was about a year long journey. I learnt that I didn't just have to write, I could voice record my chapters, I could get my recordings transcribed for an additional cost; and then my coach just dropped off the face of the universe. I tried contacting them numerous times and then came to the conclusion that something has taken precedence in their life and I need to figure out another way of getting my story out. Truly, this was a fantastic way for me to connect with many other people and find out so much more about the journey.

I learnt that voice recording my book is a fast way of getting my book written. Is it for the faint-hearted? Not at all. This part of the journey was such a healing process for me, and I uncovered details that I thought had been done & dusted years before.

I learnt that transcribing needs to be researched, as I went through an alternative country to my own and the language of my own book then had to be changed back. This can be a tedious task.

I learnt that a book can be written in many ways, in chronological order or by topic. It's your book, and it's your story. If you have an idea, map it out on sticky notes. There are your chapters. Then, devote some time to each chapter and before you know it, you will have your book.

I learnt that having a book cover to keep looking at, keep reminding you about your book, will set you up to get this book written. I used an app that provided me my book cover and a 3D version. This kept me in the moment and on target to finish my book. In fact, within months of having two book covers designed, I had all the content from both books into my publisher in just a few months. As a visual learner this is my absolute, and I got the job done.

For me, getting really honest with ME opened me up to the infinite possibilities that are out there waiting for us to grab them, hold them and mould them into our pure greatness.

As I stepped into the process I have had to look deep within and dig deep in my soul for the stories within that need to be shared with others. I truly believe that experiences are a waste of time if not shared. When the experience is shared it lessens the load, the pain heals, and it shows others that they too can find a way out of their confusion.

I was glad that I released this book first, as throughout the process I had many expectations and had them shattered and was shown so many truths. It has prepared me for the birth of my story. My story called the *Ultimate Relationship*. This is my full account of my life, real and raw. No hiding from all that has shaped me. This is me and all of me.

If you would like to work with me, you can book in at www.riasarah.com

Find me on Facebook: https://www.facebook.com/RiaSarahAuthor

Instagram: https://www.instagram.com/ria_sarah

My book *I love you, I'm Sorry* is available here: http://www.mjlpublications.com.au/product/i-love-you-i-am-sorry/

I will be officially launching this book and my newest book very soon. So please link on to my Facebook page to keep updated with this exciting event coming.

Thank you for sharing this journey with me.

Ria Sarah xx

Ria Sarah's book is a compelling tale of the events surrounding her mother's disappearance and how it brought a lifetime of grief into perspective.

As Ria puts it: "My book is about two sides of the coin. When I was 15 and left home, and how I broke my mother's heart. Then, three years ago, my mother went missing, and it shattered my world. This is my recollection of events and how I wanted to show my mum how much I loved her, how much her family loved her, and how much the rest of Australia rallied around to try to find her."

Once you pick this book up, you won't be able to put it down.

You can find Ria's book or eBook at:
http://www.mjlpublications.com.au/product/i-love-you-i-am-sorry

You Can Leave Your *Heart* On

by Sally Eberhardt

Author of *Pain-free Networking for Introverts*, connection coach, speaker and facilitator.

I'm a small business owner and big believer in the power of networking and building strong relationships.

Oh ... and I also love wild places, animals, photography, family, street art, my boyfriend, travel, reading, sports cars, writing and dining out ... not necessarily in that order. ☺

Now on with my story –

Red stilettos – powerful and determined.

Red lace gloves – cute and sassy.

Red and black lace mask – mysterious and intriguing.

Red heart-shaped chocolate box – full of sweet old-fashioned values, overflowing with LOVE.

No ... this isn't the beginning of a racy romance novel (hmmm... though maybe I will try that for my next book).

So, what do these pretty things have to do with either the writer's journey or my book *Pain-free Networking for Introverts*?

That's easy ... EVERYTHING!

These are the accessories that accompany me on my writing and book marketing odyssey.

I have photos of them on my professional author profile and take them with me to speaking engagements about either writing or networking. You see, for me, my journey as an author and networking are inextricably entwined. And each item in this little collection prompts me to share, from the heart, important insights that I have learned along the way.

Why would I say that my author's journey and networking are so integral to each other? It's not just the fact that I write about networking. The fact is that writing a book is the easy part! SELLING a book takes a lot of work, a lot of time, a lot of skills (for example, in social media and public relations) and a lot of determination.

Too many authors think their job is done when they finish writing their book. I have some news for them – if they want their book to actually get into the hands of the people who will read it (and benefit from it) rather than it sit in boxes in their garage for years, then there is still a LOT of their journey ahead of them.

Having a team to help and a mentor to advise you is invaluable – and how do you find these people? You connect with them through networking – going to events in your related field (or genre for fiction writers) and getting to know people.

Talking to people with expertise and to other authors who are ahead of you in the whole writing and book marketing game is a great way to learn from their experience. Most are very encouraging and happy to share what they have learned, and who has been really helpful to them. The more knowledge you have about people, processes, outcomes etc, the better you are able to make good decisions.

For example, my publisher was recommended to me by at least three people whom I trust. I also did my due diligence and checked out a couple of other publishers but found that their high fees did not necessarily translate into high book sales. I went with the publisher highly regarded by friends and acquaintances – they had the runs on the board and my gut instinct was to trust them. Trust your gut – it's never wrong. ☺

So, networking helped me find my publisher and book marketing mentor, my beta readers/reviewers, my best advocates and encouragers and last but by no means least – the people who BUY my book. No wonder I want to share all the opportunities that networking to build relationships can bring!

And being an introvert myself, as so many creative people are, I understand that networking is NOT easy for everyone and have written my book *Pain-free Networking for Introverts* to help take the pain out of networking and maximise the benefits.

I'm getting a bit ahead of myself here, so let's go back to the beginning of this exciting direction my life has taken ...

I always wanted to write. I loved English at school and college, enjoyed the assignments, did well – but I didn't have a burning passion to write. My spare time was taken up with horses, relationships, travel – in fact the only writing I did was letters to friends and family, and travel journals to preserve my memories. No using Facebook as a diary back then!

One of my highest values is to make this world a better place. I try to do this in a thousand ways but I also want to make a mark, leave a legacy, be a person of influence and use that power for good.

The desire to write was building in me – books are how we leverage our knowledge and reach as many people as possible as a catalyst for transformation. And I BURN to nurture transformation, to make a significant difference.

But what could I write about that would truly help others? What had I done? What struggle or disaster had I overcome? What had I achieved? What skills had I honed? What secrets did I hold? What could I contribute to make life better for others?

I asked myself these questions for a while. My life, while not ordinary, didn't seem to have the remarkableness or triumph to warrant putting pen to paper – no Oprah Winfrey or Nick Vujicic story of overcoming so much.

I had to think really hard – what topic could I impart REALLY VALUABLE information about? What did I do that many people don't – but maybe SHOULD?

The answer should have been obvious – networking. My life is so much richer for meeting people, building relationships, connecting other people to each other and so forth. Networking has brought me friendship, fun, business ventures, so many wonderful OPPORTUNITIES ... and even romance.

So many opportunities have come my way because I am out there getting to know people, staying in touch, building those relationships and helping others in any way that I can.

And I'm good at networking – really good. ☺ Because I do it from the heart.

But it wasn't always that way. I wasn't always good at it – far from it – I was terrified and clueless at first. And I didn't always do it with the love and compassion that I have now. I started networking as a way of looking for new customers. I continued networking because I gained (and gave) so much more.

At first, I had so many fears and was WAY out of my comfort zone, about a million miles out!

But you don't grow in your comfort zone – the very essence of growth lies in pushing your boundaries, expanding your horizons. And it doesn't have to be as painful as one might fear.

With starting a business, I knew I HAD to network – the survival and future of my business depended on it.

As mentioned – networking was NOT easy for me at first – it was nerve-racking, exhausting and daunting. I didn't know what to do, or say, or who to talk to, and about what; I didn't feel like I belonged ... it was a nightmare.

But I persisted because I knew that for my business, and for my SELF, I needed to network – and I learnt something from every event I attended.

I learnt how to overcome the challenges that introverts face when networking, and how to maximize the great attributes that introverts have when it comes to networking.

I want to help introverts to gain confidence, by firstly reminding them of how good they already are at networking (even though they don't realize it), and secondly, developing their competence with tips and strategies that will make them GREAT at networking ... and take the PAIN out of it.

As I mentioned – I started networking to help build my own business. I continued networking for so much more.

I have learnt what networking really is ... and isn't ... and it might surprise you.

Networking enhances my life in so many ways I could never have imagined – wonderful friendships, opportunities to be part of projects that make the world a better place, global business opportunities – and fun!

My aim is that through sharing the learnings of my networking journey as an introvert, that other people's journey will be easier and even more bountiful in every way ... whether they be introvert, extravert or somewhere in between.

Now you understand my WHY for writing my book – the driving desire to make a difference by helping others through my own experiences.

So, let's get back to those props – WHY are these items so symbolic to me and my journey? We will look at these one at a time –

RED STILETTOS

Sexy, confident, powerful, determined – UNSTOPPABLE – that's how scarlet heels make me feel. There is no slouching in high heels – you have to stand straight and proud, head up, shoulders back – ready to take on the world!

This attitude will help you in both networking and your author journey. You are going to need some grit and determination. You are going to have to be prepared to be seen and get known. It's very rare for a traditional book publisher to pick up a new author – and even then, they want you to do your own marketing.

Networking and connecting with your potential readers goes a long way in marketing. Put your heels on and start showing up at Meetups, author events, any conferences related to your topic or genre – make some connections and get to know some good people – and let them get to know you.

Stay in touch on social media, meet for coffee, see how you can help each other – there is little point in networking if you don't follow up and build on the relationship you have just started.

Does this all sound a bit daunting? GOOD! It IS daunting! But forewarned is forearmed – YOU are responsible for selling your book. Put your red stilettos on and be ready to be seen and known in the world!

RED LACE GLOVES

Hmmmm …. these are cute and sassy but maybe boxing gloves would be more appropriate …

Part of any author's journey is having their manuscript edited, critiqued and reviewed. I had friends do this for me and I was very clear on letting them know to TAKE THE GLOVES OFF!

To "take the gloves off" means that from this point forward nothing will be held back, no restraint or mercy will be shown.

I didn't want my friends to spare my feelings at all – I wanted their honest opinion and constructive criticism on anything and everything they felt needed improvement. It would do no good for them to just pat me on the back and say how wonderful my writing was – I needed their help in making this book the best that it could be.

I was also very lucky in that one of my dear friends, who was the first person I asked to run an eye over my work to see that I was on track, turned out to be an excellent editor and sent my manuscript back with a style guide and numerous very helpful edits and suggestions. She saved me some money on paying a professional (who I doubt would do the job any better) and pointed out some inconsistencies that I could then remedy before showing anyone else the manuscript. She definitely had the gloves off – and I am eternally grateful.

There are similar stories with my beta-readers – my book is what it is because they trusted enough in our relationship to be honest with me.

Which reminds me, you are going to have to take the gloves off with yourself. Be open and honest with yourself about your aims, your motives, your capabilities and what you may need help with. I had to face this with book marketing – I am confident in my writing abilities and I know a bit about marketing BUT I realised that book marketing is a whole different game that I know nothing about.

Now I am as tight with money as anyone with a few drops of Scottish blood in their veins (and I mean that with all respect – most Scots are rightly proud of their canniness and frugality), but this realisation led me to investing in my book marketing mentor. Admitting that I needed help was the first step in building a great relationship which has enriched my life by introducing me to many other authors as well as giving me the structure and tools to sell so many more copies of my book that I would have on my own.

RED AND BLACK LACE MASK

Mysterious and intriguing – who is behind that elaborate mask?

If I were to write fiction, I would leave the pretty mask on – I could hide behind characters and reveal personal stories from the safety of no one knowing or caring what part of the story was me or mine and what was made up.

But I'm not writing fiction. I'm writing about my own networking journey – and some of it is very personal. I have to drop the mask and show myself, flaws and all. This vulnerability is difficult for a woman who likes to be seen as having their act together – I'm baring my imperfections and struggles. You have to be brave to be vulnerable, but that's where people relate to you – it's where connection begins.

Much like taking the gloves off with ourselves and seeing our true selves as we are, we must drop the mask and let others see us. The following is my story of learning that it was okay to drop the mask and be ME –

"She's nice ... but she is hard to get to know" is what even people who had known me for a few years used to say about me. They were right – I was friendly, but didn't let people in. Somewhere in my life I had developed a fear that if people really knew me, they wouldn't like me. So, I didn't let them get to know me for fear of them rejecting the **real** *me. Now I can say "So what" if someone doesn't particularly like me – but I simply couldn't risk it back then – my shyness, my fear of social judgement, had a real grip on me.*

My revelation came thanks to travelling through America on Amtrak (for those not familiar with the USA, Amtrak is the interstate train system). My marriage had broken down and I pretty much ran away so I didn't have to face the aftermath of everyone telling me what I should and shouldn't do. For so long, I'd been pretending to everyone that everything was okay – and it wasn't, it **really** *wasn't. Some people could see it – but I wasn't opening up about it ... I wasn't admitting it.*

Travelling alone made it easy to meet people – even introverts need to talk to someone else occasionally – to connect with people. I played cards with kids, sat with a guy who was AWOL from the army, drank with a reformed bikie gang member and had dinner with one of the managers of Amtrak as well as meeting many other people from all walks of life.

All the people I met were so open, so honest, so encouraging and so totally non-judgemental. They shared their life stories, warts and all. They didn't hide the alcoholism, affairs, being jailed, feeling suicidal at times. They didn't sensationalize either, they just told of these things calmly as facts. They didn't boast about their life and they certainly didn't feel ashamed that their life wasn't 'perfect'. Nobody has a perfect life – what is a 'perfect life' anyway?

I heard their stories, and at last felt comfortable and accepted in telling my own. I didn't judge these people and they didn't judge me. It was such a relief and a release to realize that it's okay to drop the mask and be me.

And with the **realization** that it's okay to be me, came the **confidence** to be me. I could stop pretending everything was okay, take responsibility for my mistakes, learn and grow.

Now I am not so guarded about letting people get to know me, imperfections and all. I don't have to be perfect … I'm happy being imperfectly perfect. The best part isn't that people love me for who I am (though that is pretty awesome!) – it's that I now love me for who I am.

I still try to be the best person I can be … but that's for me, not for how anyone else might perceive me.

RED HEART-SHAPED CHOCOLATE BOX

This is my favourite prop – it makes my heart swell with love. It was given to me by my darling man for our first Valentine's

Day together and is symbolic of our decision to give our hearts to each other.

This lovely, old-fashioned, heart-shaped box also reminds me of living my values, and that networking is about giving. It's not about prospecting or making sales – it's about giving first, not keeping score, helping others and trusting that good things come to those who do good.

Since 2014, I've purposefully been attending different networking events, meeting many people, making the effort to connect and build relationships with the people whom I like and admire, WITH AN ATTITUDE PURELY OF GIVING – and with no intention in my heart or mind but to help others.

Yes, I'd been to networking events before but fairly sporadically over the previous 20 years – and to be honest, only when I had a business and I hoped I would gain new clients from networking. But now … well now is different – I truly forget about myself and am here to help others.

I never mention my business unless specifically asked – and even then, I answer very briefly and put the focus back on the other person, what they need for their business or career or life, and how I can help. I am here to GIVE.

Some people have trouble getting their head around the fact I'm not looking for anything at all for myself – I am there to connect with people and see how I (or someone I know) can help them.

Some people are under the misconception that networking is about giving to someone purely so you get something back from them. These people will soon drop you if they don't think it's likely that you will become a customer or at least give them referrals. Reciprocity is rarely that simple though – you never know when, where or who is the person who will make a huge difference in your business or life.

I'm talking about giving for the sake of giving. Forgetting about yourself and focusing on how you can help others. Showing up authentically to listen, learn and be of service.

The journey of giving has led me (and continues to lead me) down some incredibly exciting paths – and you are probably dying to know – are there rewards?

Well yes there are – many types of rewards!

Networking and connecting brings me –

opportunity | happiness | fun | purpose
satisfaction | money | love

It's the wonderful things that have happened in my life, and the wonderful things I have helped bring to the lives of others as a result of networking to give, that make me so passionate about sharing my journey.

This red heart box of cardboard and ribbon and a rose also has relevance to my writing. I write from the heart, with love and a desire to make a difference and be of service. I didn't write until I knew I had words of value and meaning that would have a positive impact on those who read them.

So, there we have it – four frivolous items that take on deeper significance when put in context. All part of my story but no prize for guessing which is closest to my heart.

You take off the gloves, drop the mask, even kick off those heels now and then ... but YOU CAN LEAVE YOUR HEART ON ☺

And in case you are wondering WHO the book is for – here is a bit of a checklist –

This book is for you if:

You want to learn how to be more comfortable in networking situations

You "should" network for your business or career

You aim to be an authority in your field

You have a product to promote

You want to make real connections with people – not just swap business cards

You want to know how to find the right place for YOU to network

You want to network so naturally that it doesn't even look (or feel) like networking

You have a dream to turn into a reality

You want to have CONFIDENCE in your networking ability

You want to reduce the stress of networking by having a plan to follow

You want RESULTS from your networking efforts

You are open to the wonderful OPPORTUNITIES that networking can bring to your business and life

You want networking to be PAIN-FREE and EFFECTIVE

You have a message to share, that will make the world a better place

One of the aims of *Pain-free Networking for Introverts* is to give you strategies so you gain CONFIDENCE via COMPETENCE.

And while the book is particularly focused on helping introverts, much of the information will of course be beneficial to ambiverts and extraverts as well.

My networking journey is continually evolving (as is yours) and I would be delighted to keep sharing my learnings with you and have opportunity to learn from you too.

Connect with me via any of these –

Facebook:
https://www.facebook.com/painfreenetworkingforintroverts

LinkedIn:
www.linkedin.com/in/sally-eberhardt-author

Twitter:

https://twitter.com/SallyEberhardt

Email:

connectwithme@sallyeberhardt.com

To buy the book *Pain-free Networking for Introverts* or read some very helpful blogs, visit my website:

www.sallyeberhardt.com

Stay in touch ... and remember – leave your heart on. ☺

Sally Eberhardt has a passion for small business, connection and collaboration.

With an eclectic background of agriculture, banking, market research and various business enterprises, Sally is equally at home talking to everyone from outback graziers to CEO's of multi-nationals.

When she first went into business for herself, Sally quickly realised the importance of networking to develop relationships and open up opportunities.

Being shy and having no clue as to what to do made networking a challenge for Sally – a challenge she embraced and that led her on her journey to networking with ease and flair. Sally shares this personal journey, along with the tips and techniques learnt, in her very soon to be published book *Pain-free Networking for Introverts*.

As Sally says:
"Networking equals opportunity. My life is living proof.

Networking has brought so much to my life – wonderful business connections and referrals of course … but also friendships, travel, being part of projects that make the world a better place, and even romance. In short, networking is about OPPORTUNITIES – DON'T MISS OUT!"

Facebook: Sally Eberhardt – Author

Email: connectwithme@sallyeberhardt.com

Website: www.sallyeberhardt.com

POWER MARKETING
An Aussie Guide to Business Growth

Jennifer Lancaster

A Passion for Marketing

by Jennifer Lancaster

Who are you?

I'm a copywriter, book author and editor who loves to share good value. As author of *Power Marketing, How to Start a Freelance Business* and *Create Your New Life of Abundance*, among others, it's apparent that I am focussed on personal brand, promotion, saving, as well as personal growth and positivity.

What is personal brand marketing?

Marketing is, at its simplest, getting the word out about you to your ideal audience. If I've learned anything in the past 20 years, it's that it's no good hiding your light under a bushel. My book and blogs were like a testing ground for personal brand marketing, mainly because I was scared stiff of cold calling. And who wouldn't be – it's rubbish.

I've learned that it's more powerful to put yourself in the spotlight instead of just a company name. Think of Virgin, it would be nothing but a red logo and a price focus without Richard Branson.

A vibrant personal brand with good graphics and a clear message will form the foundation. Add a dash of personality and a piece of your soul and you'll be on your way.

What product or service do you offer?

At Power of Words, I now offer insights into what's missing from a business's online marketing and website. As a copywriter, I might consult personally, help with style guides, and then write better website content and articles.

You might be thinking… what the heck is a style guide? A style guide is a set of standards for the writing and design of documents. It ensures consistency across an organisation's documents and it guides in the usage of visual composition, typography, and language/tone.

Of course, my focus is more on the message, brand proposition, and the way it's expressed (the tone). While design elements need to be consistent and thought-through, it's the heart and purpose of the organisation and their unique value proposition that must somehow be carried into the website copy.

Due to my background in writing books, I'm also development editor for two authors who are writing their book. Sometimes authors get stuck or cannot see their writing patterns, and so I help get the book clear and targeted to their reader.

Who is your ideal client?

The service business with a leader looking for differentiation, who needs support in their messaging. Or if the person is interested in putting their theories and experiences into a book, then I would help through my coaching and book development program.

> *Which of their concerns/challenges/desires do you address and how do you achieve that?*

I've found most business people write about themselves, not their audience, so I like to turn it around and investigate the hidden desires and needs of the target persona. Sometimes that person is me! For instance, once when I wrote copy for a roofing company, I could use my own concerns in the copy as I was considering my own roof replacement.

Nearly everyone with a website is concerned with attracting and warming up leads – but to make a website really work is not an easy, once-off thing. If you're in it on your own, then it might take 2-3 years to crack decent levels of traffic. By blogging and reaching out to others via social media platforms, you can build your network and website visitor levels.

Many small business owners are still trying to advertise instead of educate. They can remedy this malfunction with a lead magnet offer. A lead magnet is any piece of content that's valuable for ideal visitors that you offer in order to get email (or phone) leads. It allows for a drip email series that if written warmly, then helps gain trust in the spokesperson and brand.

> *How did you come to write your book?*

My first book in 2008 was called *Sack Your Financial Planner*. I wrote it because I was angry at being scammed, just like many others, however I mainly focussed on positive actions, like 'minding the gap' (saving) and using leverage. I was also planning my family's finances at the time.

I have found through my life's up-down financial journey that it's important to keep your head in the right space. There are many tips for this in *'Create Your New Life of Abundance'* – along with the background of positive psychology.

For *Power Marketing*, it was a case of combining all the marketing tips that I learned while copywriting for businesses, writing a marketing blog, and learning SEO. I also heard some woeful marketing tales, so I used these as 'what not to do' learning points. The book changed multiple times, but it continues to be a source of promotional ideas, even for me.

> *What tip, tool or pearl of wisdom can you share that would help our readers to help themselves to become successful authors?*

It's important to look out for *Joint Venture partnerships*, which I'll talk about in a moment.

Getting a niche blog, with your name on it, helps set things up... and scheduling related social media postings consistently helped me to gain more visibility. Scheduling means your time is leveraged, and for this I used Zoho Social, which is free at their base level.

My optimisation knowledge helped to rank my blog nationally, and you can find out how to do this too by reading/listening to Neil Patel's blog or by using SEOMoz.

Intuit (maker of Quickbooks) contacted me to joint venture on their graphic campaign about tools for freelancers. So, I wrote the post 'Tools of the Freelance Trade', containing their link, but was surprised to find 240 people had shared my book page as well.

To attract joint ventures, you need to make friends in the niche you write about. A great way to do this is to review industry leaders' books on your own blog. The author of many great titles on book marketing, Penny Sansevieri, also shared my book review post and that got a small influx too.

Whenever you find someone you admire, go to LinkedIn. With LinkedIn, you can see interest groups of your followers as well as their updates. Interact as you read.

Why is this important?

While it's cool to connect with those influencers, and it gets some leverage, you need to create your own valuable posts and videos or audios too. With time, people might reckon *you* are the influencer in your market if you work on it enough.

Plenty of times, new authors expect the world to beat a path to their book... but it's not like that, readers have to be teased into it with snippets of your book's content and other tips.

If you take it a step further with LinkedIn and help those in your circles, they are more likely to read your feed, and if interested in your book launch message, read your book. From there, they might be interested in consulting with you or doing a course you made. And that's where you can really leverage your wonderful writing.

> *How can your reader learn more from you? Where can they find you and what else do you have to offer them?*

Many readers may be interested in book marketing, personal branding and self-publishing; if so they can visit www.jenniferlancaster.com.au/blog. Besides information on editing styles and the self-publishing process, there are instructions on how to make an author blog and other resources, so it's jam-packed with information for new authors. Google loved this apparently, and many blog readers have contacted me for more help or just to give their opinion.

You can see that it is separated into topic categories. These are natural sub-topics of self-publishing, except for personal finance. The more obvious it is that you go deep into your topic, the more your blog will attract new readers. To keep readers, I use an authentic voice and share my own current experiences and learning.

Freebies! Please sign up on my blog for a free niche marketing course and monthly marketing tips.

For Business Builders:

Based on my experience in website creation, I recently created a marketing program. Perhaps you can use this as a guide for your marketing. I believe a business builder must go through these nine steps before the magic happens.

The *Differentiator Program* comprises:

1. Analyse Audience, Outline Personas
2. Define What Your Service Enables
3. Get the Message Right
4. Brand Representation – tone, story, and values
5. Develop Content of Relevance
6. Technical SEO and Onsite SEO
7. Fix Follow-up and Qualify Prospects
8. Article Marketing / Videos
9. Track Metrics and Goal Conversions

Visit Powerofwords.com.au for more information on the steps.

If you follow these steps, your business will have the best-practice structure of businesses like King Content, Amplify

Agency, and The Naked CEO. HubSpot is another place for content marketing insight.

Another thing to consider is whether your style is more suited to voice, visual, or the written word. So, for a writer, blogging and writing books comes naturally. For a visual person, photography on Instagram and creative videos would be your style. For a gifted verbal communicator, conversation through a podcast and public speaking would suit. If you try to cover off everything, then nothing will fly... but stick to your natural talents and your message will take off.

Jennifer Lancaster is the author of *Power Marketing: An Aussie Guide to Business Growth*, *Create your New Life of Abundance*, and more. Marketing is her other love. Jen wants to leave a legacy as a helpful writer, simplifying difficult concepts and providing top value always.

Jennifer Lancaster
Power of Words
Author, editor, and copywriter
0403125038

Professional Member, Institute of Professional Editors (IPEd)

Portfolio:
http://powerofwords.com.au/portfolio

Publishing Blog:
https://jenniferlancaster.com.au/blog

Author of: *Power Marketing*, *How to Control Your Financial Destiny*, *How to Start a Freelance Business*, and *Create your New Life of Abundance*.

A SIMPLE DRIVE HOME

LISA CONSTANTINE

Tragedy and Grit
by Lisa Constantine

Who wants to write about tragedy? Tragedy happens every day. But I have, because I boast learned life lessons I never knew and put simply wish to share with you, the reader.

I took back the power which was taken away from me. I came to understand this is called 'personal power'; and I am not a psychiatrist, psychologist or counsellor. This 'personal power' gives you the freedom and choice of how you want to live your life.

Personal power means having a deep sense of empowerment. It is an inner strength and confidence which comes forward through the toughest times. It is the ability to take decisive and deliberate action.

I realized I had a personal choice to be a victim of this tragic car accident and the permanent injuries I sustained, or I could react in a positive way. I had every right to blame and resent what happened to me, but I made a conscious decision to switch my energy into recovery, rehabilitation and survival strategies.

At first, I gave myself permission to shed tears, be outraged and mournful, and I had my own pity party – *why me*?

Trauma and tragedy are very real, but I finally comprehended that I had to refrain from feeling powerless and pull to the forefront my own personal power. It began with small steps and tiny mindset changes. It became all about perception.

I do not mean blind optimism, saying I am fine when I certainly was not. I mean realistic optimism, which is hoping for the best but being prepared for the worst. I knew the long road of physical and emotional challenges ahead. I was not naïve, but I had to have stamina and resolution.

Each of us encounters hard times, hurt feelings, heartache, physical and emotional pain. The key is to realize it is not what happens to you that matters, it is how you choose to respond. You have a choice. You can choose self-encouragement and self-motivation, or you can choose self-defeat or seek sympathy.

Many people think they are not responsible for how they feel. People think circumstances or other individuals make them feel a certain way. For instance: 'He or she made me so angry'. There is a difference between complaining and problem solving; when you vent to your friends, family or co-workers it keeps you focused on the problem and prevents you from creating a solution. The whining implies you have no personal power over your situation and attitude, but you can control your perspective, attitude, reaction, feelings, thoughts and beliefs.

Attitude can be your best friend or your worst enemy, and your perception can have enormous influence over your actions. To adjust your perspective to see your life through positive lenses means that no matter what life throws your way this outlook is a likeable option.

I also learned the term 'growth mindset', which is when you believe you can improve your life with effort and consistency. The opposite of a 'growth mindset' is a 'fixed mindset'. You believe you are who you are, and you cannot change. This creates problems when you're challenged, because anything which appears to you for you to handle is bound to make you feel hopeless and overwhelmed.

A fixed mind-set means challenges are avoided, obstacles are given up upon, effort is not worth it, and criticism is ignored.

A growth mind-set means challenges are embraced, obstacles are a temporary setback, effort equals mastery and criticism is a means for self-improvement.

Our attitude is what other people see of you. Since your inner worlds are hidden, it is important to remember we all have a public face we show to people and a private life they will never see. It is your position which expresses your disposition, and it is so visible that your character makes or breaks how you are received.

Attitude is more than a sunny outlook on life. It is a straight forward way of changing negative habits. It is a true belief that good things will come in spite of the bad things.

It is about intentionality. It is about knowing who you are. It is about having a handle on your passions, abilities and weakness. One of the most valuable things you can do is find out and define what your purpose in life is. Intentional living is defining *why* you do what you do.

Living an intentional life does not mean you rid your life of all tribulation and suffering. We often struggle to heal the wounds in your lives. These are hurts and bitterness from the past which can continue to haunt us. It is about controlling your thoughts, feelings and emotions to be more competent.

Living intentionally means you face your life head on; persevering through misfortune and by practicing this it can make you stronger and shape you. The only person that will remain constant in your life is you.

Perseverance is another factor in living intentionally, because the outcome is you start preparing, planning and aligning your time with your most significant objectives. In a nutshell, perseverance is the act of persisting to do something in spite of challenges, obstacles and disappointments. Highly successful people have a morning ritual routine and are intentional with their time.

Perseverance in your life is an essential quality if you are to realize your goals and achieve success.

There are six steps to improve your perseverance:

1. Establish what it is you desire;
2. Have a step by step plan to achieve your goals;
3. Work towards a manageable timeframe for your goals;
4. Identify obstacles, strategies and contingency plans;
5. Execute self-control to prevent distractions or being side tracked; and
6. Encourage self-growth and self-improvement.

To put it simply; you start to minimize the amount of decisions you make on trivial issues. This also includes happiness.

Happiness is never dependent on anything external. It is a personal preference. I am happy because I choose to be happy.

Trying to live a happy life is not denying negative emotions or pretending to be joyful all the time. We all encounter adversity and it is completely natural for us to feel anger, sadness and frustration.

Outside behaviours and influences have the power to trigger off negative thoughts, but this can only happen if you allow it to. Change the way your respond to the triggers and consequently they can have no effect on inflicting any kind of misery upon you. Sometimes, being happy is not easy to do, but if you consciously make the effort it can help your state of mind.

It can be difficult to take an honest look at yourself, because most of us lack a healthy self-knowledge and self-image. It is a simple fact that we do not make time for introspection. Our technology-driven lives make it complicated to reflect on our behaviour or our conjectures and functioning. Without reflection, you can struggle. We tend to live our lives on autopilot. We all have weaknesses but learning about yourself helps you recognize how you can do things more toughly or differently, and this is *why:* the fundamental reason happiness is important. It is vital to our own goals in life and can assist in your personal ambitions.

By nurturing a positive, confident self-image, you will find it easier to be introspective in examining your life, learn about yourself and make intrinsic decisions. Prosperity is a mindset and a series of habits tied around this intellect to flourish and prosper.

When you know what is important to you, then you can use your life aims as a compass for each decision you make, and by doing this deliberately you will uncover your values. It is when you face your choices with courage and confidence that you open yourself to a fulfilling path of your own design.

Your thoughts determine your actions. When you raise your personal standards, it is not being an ego-manic. Your personal standards are intricately intertwined with your level of self-esteem and self-respect. Most people never recognize what they are capable of because they think small and lack self-efficacy. When you raise your personal standards, you are reminding yourself *why* you are deciding to do it and what you are going to do.

It is about the observation of your actions.

Here are four action steps:

1. *Awareness* – a critical first step toward mind set action.
2. *Acceptance* – accept the situation and what you can and can't control.
3. *Adjustment* – what adjustments can I make to improve the situation?

4. *Action* – take action consciously and intelligently.

Good choices are generated in your mind, and it's granted that other life factors come into play, but your love for others, your desire to peruse personal interests and the motivation to achieve something is what you deem important.

Nevertheless, the more your mind is absent from the choice making process, the more likely you are to follow the urge and make a choice without acknowledging its impact on your life. I believe this is called 'self-accountability'.

Self-accountability means making your own decision, and by doing so this allows you to be responsible for the result of your decision whether it is a positive move or not.

Life is like a road. There are long and short roads, smooth and rocky roads. Just like roads there are corners, detours and crossroads in life and these crossroads I believe are the choices you make.

To prevent your past from defining your future, you need to put the past firmly where it belongs, and that is behind you. The past can be a handicap. It is by thinking differently that you can steer your future in the direction you want to go.

You need to have a classic victor inclination, because a triumph perspective helps you create an easy integration work and lifestyle balance.

A positive mindset involves attitudes and core beliefs that form the foundation of who you are and how you approach life. This beneficial view determines boundaries you set with others and yourself, the choices we mindfully make and the actions we execute.

Self-development is also about a productive mindset, because growing and developing your mind and your emotional resilience increases your self-confidence and self-worth. Self-development requires your commitment to life-long learning and progressively and consistently acquiring the necessary knowledge, experience and skills to help you propel yourself forward towards your individual goals.

Another point to consider is when you compare yourself to others – this is a victim mentality notion. Avoid victim-mode of impeaches, pointing fingers or externalizing the problems and experiences towards something or someone else.

We all share fear and doubts which creep in, both rational and irrational. It's human nature to want to be liked and appreciated but worrying about what other people think of you can become a trap. It is when you become obsessed with other people's opinion of you; you forget your own personality, thoughts and actions.

You have to know who you are as a person, because there is no one like you on this earth and there never will be. *Why would you want to live someone else's life when you have* your life to live? Life is about building your own dreams and achieving your goals. To be the best version of yourself.

Choosing your thoughts carefully can change your mindset. It is all about being mindful of how you reach a decision and what concept pattern you need to break or change.

Trauma, tragedy, suffering, hardships, difficulties and illness cannot be changed; these are facts which have occurred, but you can control how you look at the situation. The key is awareness.

When you choose the road less travelled of not allowing tough circumstances to hold you back from living life to the full, things can be difficult. It is a daily intentional decision, when it would be easier for you to wallow in self-pity and indulge in victimhood.

Our most precious commodities are not smartphones, 3D televisions, brand new cars or even our big and impressive houses or ordering online. It is our purpose in life. Purpose is your *why?* It drives your actions. It fuels your passion. It means living your life in an intentional way. Living in an intentional way gives your life a sharper focus. Your *why* is what keeps you going when life gets tough.

To find your *why*, ask yourself three questions:

1. What is my reason for getting up in the morning?
2. What do I want more of in my life?
3. Where am I trying to get to?

It is also termed your 'calling', which is your sense of meaning in life. This is your passion and gives your life purpose and fills you with a sense of vitality that makes everything simple and enjoyable. Your calling is how you make a difference to your life and others. Your calling is your life's work. It is your legacy. To find out what you have a passion for and to pursue that zeal, is to find the vehicle you'll use to contribute your greatness to the world. If you take the time to work on yourself to remove negative influences from your life, you find that you have more time for things that bring you joy.

It is also about living a life of gratitude. I believe this choice of gratitude is what makes it possible for you to still live your life healthy, well, wild and free, even in the middle of the hardest circumstances. It is important to believe in your mind and heart that you are worthy of love, respect and kindness.

Being grateful doesn't imply you're got your rose-coloured glasses permanently on. Nor does it mean everything is necessarily wonderful. It simply indicates that you're aware of your blessings, appreciate the small things and acknowledge all you do have.

Gratitude lets you pause for a moment to reflect on something you have in our life right now, instead of always striving for objects like a new dress, new car or the house renovation. Gratitude is indeed one of the most powerful states of mind you can adapt.

None of us are born resilient. I believe it is something you become and learn. It is human nature to resist change particularly when a shift comes in the form of adversity or challenges. Change in life is inevitable and developing the trait of resilience helps you not only to survive, but to learn to grow. When you give up the quest to learn resilience you accept vulnerability, determinism and defeat.

A victor faces challenges and weakness. Victors prepare their mind every day to be set to the take of what needs to be done in order to achieve their goals down the road. The preparation to achieve is a huge part of the victor's inner operating system. This intellect of a victor takes hard work, self-discipline, regimentation, consistency and compliance to the process.

Another factor in this life puzzle is self-respect. Self-respect allows you to be you. It is about allowing your individuality and uniqueness to appear when you respect yourself, and this has a chain reaction of others respecting you.

Self-respect requires you to be introspective, sincere, open, broad-minded and fair. It does not mean you are inconsiderate or disrespectful of others. It means you will not let others define you or make decisions for you which you should make for yourself.

The most important two goals in life are personal tranquillity and peace of mind; however, these objectives can be difficult to attain if you are trying to live by someone else's rules. To have a liberating life, you must be yourself. This is *why* it is easier to see what you want in life and what is significant to you when you are yourself.

Other people's perceptions can be based on their past programming and conditioning. If you worry about what other people think of you then you are living in their reality, not your own. Be different, be you, you do not need to follow the herd or crowd and you learn to ignore the crap. Life is a self-fulfilling prophecy. You can steer your future in the direction you want to go. Your decisions are your ultimate power.

I believe it is preferable to be resourceful because procrastination can be a time waster. You can develop a resourceful mindset if you are to be willing to constantly improve yourself. Resourcefulness makes you extra self-reliant. Resourcefulness gives you the ability to find and use available resources to achieve your aims.

I believe another factor is critical thinking. It is about you knowing who can help you and what you need. To gain resourcefulness requires you to have an open mind and focusing on the process and learning opportunities to see options, and to turn your thoughts into actions and disregarding less menial stuff.

Dreams not do work unless you do the hard yards; therefore, instead of coming home after work to watch television, get to cultivating on your true desires. If you spend your days on high quality activities, your vision and wish will no longer be pipe dreams.

My trauma sent me on a path I would have never have found otherwise. Trauma is not a free pass to avoid pain and suffering, but it gave me the opportunity to reflect, to search for meaning in my life to ultimately be a better version of me.

I realized my own resilience and my priorities changed for the better. I turned my bitterness into better by getting into the now moment by concerning myself with current opportunities, my goals and my future.

My name is Lisa Constantine. I am a Brisbane writer, best-selling author and inspirational public speaker. My book *A Simple Drive Home* is my compelling story of my recovery after a P-plater nearly claimed my life. Life can change in a second.

My *why* is, I simply want to share my story, because there were days I did not want to even brush my hair or even have a shower or get out of bed. The orthopaedic surgeons wanted to amputate my right knee from the knee down. In the medical world, this was the worst structural damage to a right knee in Australia. My story is an uplifting and in parts humorous memoir that reminds us to live life to the fullest. My recovery is still on-going.

I am not represented in my book as an exceptional person but rather as an ordinary young woman who was in the wrong place at the wrong time.

My ideal client includes anyone experiencing or exposed trauma, tragedy, surgeries, physical injury, rehabilitation, illness, heartache or a life changing experience.

My book is 20 years in the making, but if I did not write my inspirational story when I did, it would not be the book it is today. My book started on the backs of envelopes, napkins and bits of scrap paper.

I think anyone who has the determination and desire to write their own story should. It is simply to just start writing and remember there are many drafts before your masterpiece. It is important to write your narrative scoop, because we all have a story inside us. Reading a story is knowledge and sharing with the world.

To learn more about me: www.lisaconstantine.com

www.lisaconstantine.com

Lisa Constantine is an author, writer and inspirational speaker. In her powerful book *A Simple Drive Home* Lisa reveals her compelling journey from victim to victor after a P-plater took out her car in a horrific car accident that nearly claimed her life.

Orthopaedic surgeons wanted to amputate Lisa's right leg from the knee down. Lisa was left with permanent disabilities. Today, Lisa's recovery is still on-going. Her inspiring story is a reminder of how life can change in a split second, that every day should be lived with intention, and the importance in life to know who you are.

Her book is an autobiography plus a personal development tool.

Lisa believes that experiencing trauma is not uncommon, but resilience takes time to learn, understand and master.

Melly S
The Story Collector

10 Winning Tactics to Market Your Book with Video

by Melly Stewart

'Why do so many people think marketing their book is expensive and complicated?' I thought to myself as I poured the hot water into my coffee cup. 'How do I get the message across that it really isn't? Maybe I have to lay the stats and facts on people.'

That angle just felt awkward. Just as awkward as the slow walk towards my office with my overflowing coffee cup spilling everywhere. I really should be better at this by now.

As I sat down at my desk and slopped even more coffee everywhere (damn it!) and mopped it up with the end of my dressing gown (hey, don't judge. I wash it!), I thought, 'Stop it! Stop talking to yourself and start talking with "the people" instead.'

So here I am. Talking to you.

Why do you think marketing your book is expensive and complicated?

You know everything you need fits into the palm of your hand, right? Thanks to technology, we have the power to create amazing, high quality videos to market our books and business right there on our phone.

Are you rushing over to grab your phone? No? Why do you hesitate?

I get it. When we stand in front of that camera we have a tonne of negative thoughts running through our heads about why we CAN'T use video for marketing. I have no doubt as soon as I said video that voice has piped up and has been whispering to you:

"I don't like the way I look."

"I sound funny."

"No one wants to hear me stumbling over words."

"I have no idea how to use video."

Let's address the first 3 thoughts right now with a little bit of tough love. (I promise it's gentle tough love. Kinda like Mum's tap on the hand when you reach for the cookie jar before dinner.)

Ask yourself the following question: Why did you write your book in the first place?

Seriously, ask yourself.

I'll wait.

Done? Good. Like most people, I am sure the underlying message of your response will be to inspire others. You wrote your book to inspire others.

So, really, after you have poured your heart and soul into it, at the end of the day (so to speak), your book is not about you. It's about using your story, your circumstances or your knowledge to inspire SOMEONE ELSE.

You wouldn't go to all that trouble of writing and publishing a book to leave it on a shelf for no one to ever read. That's what journals are for. You did it for someone else to pick up, absorb the words on that page, and to then take action based on those words. You did it for someone else.

Therefore, once you have written and published your book… (and here's the tough love…)

IT IS NO LONGER ABOUT YOU!

(Did you feel the slap?)

Once you have written and published your book, it is no longer about you. Yes, it contains your stories. Yes, it contains your words and memories. But it is no longer about you. YOUR role in the book is done. It is now entirely about your reader.

And guess what?

The same goes for using video to market your book (and/or business).

When it's time to stand in front of that camera and market your book, it is no longer about you. It is 100% about the person who will one day pick it up and be inspired by your symphony of words. (Ok, so maybe 99% about them, because hey, you're important too!)

Now, don't skim over what I've just written or take it too lightly. This is HUGE if you truly let it into your heart and subconscious. This little pearl of wisdom transformed my business and my life. When this truth finally settled for me, it gave me a sense of untold freedom, and along with that came a sense of security and comfort. Why?

No one cared that my teeth are a bit crooked… because it wasn't about me.

No one cared I permanently sounded like I had a cold… because it wasn't about me.

No one cared that I stumbled on my words occasionally… because it wasn't about me.

IT WASN'T ABOUT ME!

I'll finish off my coffee while I wait for that little truth bomb to sink in for you.

Now that crosses off your first 3 complaints, let's jump into the last one.

"I have no idea how to use video."

Ok, I will take this as an acceptable concern because yes, there are some technical elements to using video that if you don't get quite right can hurt your marketing efforts instead of getting people's attention and driving sales. (And side note: if I hear you even mutter, "I need a better phone", that tough love is going to come out again, alright? Because these tips work regardless of the device you are using. Got it?)

Let's dive into the **10 Winning Tactics to Market Your Book With Video**.

Winning Tactic Number 1

With the ever-increasing amount of content being shoved in our faces on social media, we are very quick to judge whether a video is worthy of our time. Unfortunately, this means that 99% of people are going to make a split-second decision based on what they see. So, it makes sense the number one winning tactic is make your video look good. How? It's all in getting your lighting right. And honestly, it is much easier than it seems.

The quick rule when it comes to lighting for your videos is: Light in front of you. Not behind you.

Our phone sensor is a tricky thing and most phones really can't tell whether you are trying to make YOU look good or if you trying to make the scenery look good. The phone automatically assumes whatever is brightest is what you are trying to video. This means, if the light is behind you, typically you will appear dark (and sometimes blurry) and everything behind you looks really bright and crisp. If you are in this situation, simply turn around the other way to make sure the light is brighter in front of you.

Now, if you find yourself pulling a squishy "Arrghhh my eyes! The light! It burns!" face (you know, the face you pull when the sun is in your eyes), move around a bit more so you're not looking directly into glare or the burning ball of gas that heats up our solar system. Problem solved.

Winning Tactic Number 2

Winning Tactic number 2 is all about how you position your camera. General rule of thumb is: landscape mode only (that's your video longways). I say general rule because there are some social media platforms who prefer portrait mode (tall image), however I firmly believe it is only a matter of time before they conform to landscape mode.

Why?

We have two eyes that sit side by side so we visually process more in landscape mode than we do in portrait mode and to further state my case with an exclamation mark and a very poignant full stop; Have you ever seen a movie shot in portrait? No? I rest my case.

While also on the subject of positioning your camera, can we forget about the famous "selfie" angle please? Psychologically speaking, by holding the camera high you are making yourself look smaller in the video. "Great idea!" I hear you thinking. The problem with this is that the human psyche then translates this camera angle into, "Oh I'm looking down on you, therefore I am above you. Therefore, I know more than you."

Don't believe me? Ask a vertically challenged friend how they (sometimes) get treated in a room full of tall people. Go on. I dare you!

The opposite is also true if you record from a lower angle with the camera looking up at you. While you give the viewer an awesome idea of when you last blew your nose, you are also giving the perception that you are bigger than them and therefor know more than them (and not in a good way!).

Position your camera at eye level so the person watching your video feels like they are talking WITH you. Oh, and please make sure to look at the camera when you are talking, so the viewer feels like they are getting eye contact. The camera on your phone is usually the little dot TO THE SIDE OF THE SCREEN. When you look at yourself talking on the screen, from the viewers perspective, it actually feels like you aren't quite looking at them. Ever have a conversation with someone and they can't quite look you in the eye? It's quite off putting, isn't it?

Quick Tip: If you can't help but look at yourself (I get it. I know you're gorgeous!), then here is a quick hack for you. Place a sticky note with a big arrow pointing at the camera over the screen so not only can you no longer see yourself, it's a very clear visual reminder to look at the camera.

Winning Tactic Number 3

Uno, Dos, Tres. Really quick, but vitally important tip. Stabilise your footage please! You are not shooting the latest blockbuster, so there is really no need to see you running down the street with your footage jumping around everywhere. Not unless half way through recording you start getting chased by a 100-pound gorilla for no particular reason... because in that case, it is justified. Otherwise, just use a tripod. Please! (And by the way, I have no idea how much gorillas weigh, so don't laugh at the weight of my gorilla... unless I get it spot on, in that case, carry on.)

Winning Tactic Number 4

We've found the right light, we've positioned the camera, and we've stabilised it. Now it's time to frame yourself in the shot. If you're thinking Madonna's famous Vogue face framing dance moves right now, you are on the right track. She really was on a winner with those moves. Essentially, we want to see you, not the entire room, but we also don't want you to be so close that we can see the pores on your nose.

The general rule is: bottom of the image should be roughly nipple height (insert girly giggle here. Yes, I said nipple), and the top of the image should finish with a small gap at the top of your head. This shows just enough body language so it's not just your facial expressions doing all the "talking" for you and allows room for you to move around naturally without cutting your head off.

Why don't we crop it in closer? One. You could end up looking like a floating bobble head if you are in too close. Two. A huge and rising percentage of videos are watched online without sound, which means at some point you are going to have to look at subtitles (But we'll save that for another time). All you need to know for now is that we need to leave room for those subtitles to fit in, and unless you want it to look like you are (literally) eating your words, leave some room at the bottom.

Quick Tip: Oh, and another quick tip for you! If you keep yourself positioned in the centre of the video, you can edit the video into a square format easily for multiple social media platforms without cutting off an ear or half your face. You're welcome!

Winning Tactic Number 5

Now, while I did say practically no one is watching videos with the sound on, here's a little catch 22 for you. You need the sound to be able to get subtitles. And, on the rare occasion when someone DOES want to listen to the sound, they will tune out very quickly if it's not clear and easily audible. I've stuffed around with lots of different options in the past when it comes to getting the sound right with your phone (and spent way too much money in the process), and the best option, which I highly recommend for everyone, is to get your backside over to JB-HiFi and pick yourself up a Rode smartLav.

The hardest part of using it is figuring out how to get it out of the box. Once you've gotten it out of the box (scissors may be required), it plugs straight into your phone and just like that, near to perfect sound.

This works so well that I've even used this exact set-up when recording interviews at a Red-Carpet Gala event in a crowded room full of people and I was STILL able to hear the person clearly in the recording.

So, let's see where we are at…

You've got your lighting on point. Check.

You've positioned the camera right. Check.

You've stabilised it with a tripod. Check.

You've framed yourself in the shot. Check.

The sound is on and working perfectly. Check.

And now you look super strained (maybe even constipated) because behind the scenes you are stuck pulling some super awkward yoga move to get yourself in the exact right position.

Winning Tactic Number 6

Adjust and re-adjust and re-adjust again until you feel comfortable.

That's it.

Winning Tactic Number 7

If you have been implementing these tips as you go, you will now be looking at yourself in the camera, looking amazing (you sexy thing), and the realisation that you must now say something has jumped into your mind. Now you're making little nervous giggles as you seem to have lost the ability to speak.

So, keeping in mind we only have a split second to get people's attention so they WANT to stick around and watch your video, winning tactic number 7 is highly important. Grab their attention immediately!

Don't stuff around with a meek and mild, "Hi, I'm Melly." Don't muck around fixing your hair or moving into a better position. (Not that you will need to if you follow Tactics 1 – 6. Which I know you will because I'm stuck in your head now, right?)

Just jump into it and grab their attention IMMEDIATELY!

If you have a big personality, then make a grand gesture. Wave at the camera. Jump up and down a bit. Do whatever feels comfortable to get the viewers' attention. Have some fun with it.

Then give your viewer a reason to keep watching. A short and sharp sentence or question so they can say, "Yes, I want to watch this."

"Want to know how to turn your videos from zero to hero?"

"What should you really do to make your videos look great?"

"The truth is, you are not the only person who doesn't know how to use video."

There are so many different ways of grabbing people's attention and, as an author, this is where you really have a superpower that most others don't. Could you pose them a question? Or make a bold statement that throws them off! Or completely confuse them by stating something that has nothing to do with what you are actually talking about and then in a round-about way lead it all together again.

Winning Tactic Number 8

You've got their attention. Now what? Winning tactic number 8 is the biggest part of your video and one that I have built my entire business around. Why? Because no-one is doing this right, and it is the secret to attracting your ideal people to you and buying from you with very little effort on your part! And the best part? As an author, you have this superpower within you, ready to be unleashed…

But, before we go into detail on Winning tactic number 8 (Yup, I'm going to make you wait a little bit longer. I know, I know, I suck. You'll thank me for it later though) …

Winning Tactic Number 9

Winning tactic number 9 is about finishing off your video by leaving your viewer with a very clear message. Something that sticks in their head. A message that they can repeat to others without too much thought, because let's face it, we barely remember what we had for breakfast yesterday let alone what someone said in that random video we saw yesterday. (It was coffee, by the way, according to yesterday's dirty cup sitting on my desk in front of me right now. Am I the only one who forgets to take their coffee cups to the sink?)

I will admit, it took me a while to figure out my message, and it wasn't until a conversation with a business associate that it really clicked for me. Here's how that conversation went:

"If I meet someone who I think needs your services, Mel, what do I say to them?"

"Hmmm, you could say, "Melly can help you create video storytelling strategies that easily connect your stories with your ideal clients so sales and opportunities find you"."

"What? How am I meant to remember that?" Blank stare directed squarely at me.

Now imagine me sitting there feeling like I had just been slapped across the face. I had been working for months on getting those exact words right to encapsulate everything I did. Months, I tell you! MONTHS! But damn, she was so right!

How was anyone meant to remember that when I could barely remember it myself? Finally, I took a deep breath, and this came out: "At the core of it, I help people grow their businesses with video storytelling. I guess you could say I'm their video go-to gal."

And just like that, my short, sharp and punchy message was born.

I'll leave you to ponder on that one for a bit and apply it to your own book (or business).

Winning Tactic Number 10

So, you've done an entire video, your viewer has stuck around long enough to watch the whole thing, but now what? This is where our final tip Tactic number 10 comes in, and that is our Call To Action.

What do you WANT them to do?

Do you want them to call you? Do you want them to send you an email? Do you want them to buy your book?

Now, if you've said all of the above, where can you send them so they get ALL of that info at once? (If you said website... GOLD STARS FOR YOU!)

Keep your call to action very minimal and short so it is very clear what you want your viewer to do. Essentially, this becomes your sign off on every single video you do, and while it takes practice to become comfortable saying it, once you've got it, it just rolls off the tongue.

"I'm MellyS, and I'm your video go-to gal. If you want to know how to grow your business with video storytelling, then jump over to my website: mellys.com.au."

WINNING TACTICS RECAP

Tactic Number 1: Light in front, not behind.

Tactic Number 2: Position your camera landscape and at eye level.

Tactic Number 3: Stabilise your footage.

Tactic Number 4: Frame yourself in the shot. (Nipples, people. Nipples! Yes, you may giggle.)

Tactic Number 5: Use a microphone.

Tactic Number 6: Adjust until 1 – 5 works for you.

Tactic Number 7: Grab your viewers' attention.

Tactic Number 8: (We'll get to that in a moment. Just hold your horses, ok?)

Tactic Number 9: Wrap up your video with a short and memorable message.

Tactic Number 10: Finish it with a clear and precise Call to Action.

Winning Tactic Number 8 (for reals this time)

Ok, I hear you. You want to know what that elusive Tactic Number 8 is, right? (If you were really paying attention, you would have picked up on it already. Yup, I've literally said what tactic number 8 is multiple times so far. Just saying!)

Tactic number 8 is where, being an author and having a gift with words, is going to be highly beneficial for you. It's something that most businesses have to LEARN how to do, because unlike for you it is not a natural gift. Hence why I have built my entire business on teaching this skill to entrepreneurs.

So, what is it?

Winning Tactic number 8 is… storytelling.

People crave stories. We crave the emotional connection we get when we hear a great story. It's why we ask people where they went and what they did. It's why your book needed to be written. It's the fundamental element to human connection on a deeper soul level.

And here's the icing on the cake (mmmm, cake): the power of this, as a marketing tool, is that stories naturally attract the right people to us. By sharing our stories and sharing our emotions and thoughts through these stories, we are giving our viewer a chance to know, like and respect us. What does this mean for your bottom line? Only once someone knows, likes and respect us will they ever even consider buying from you, and you want people to buy your book, right?

The winning tactics of video can be easily taught, but the depth of your video truly lies in your ability to tell a good story, and you know what? That part is just naturally a part of you. Lucky you!

Now look, I could go on into a tonne of detail when it comes to what stories to tell and where to tell them, but I'm running out of allocated pages and I seriously want lunch now. (I had to mention cake, didn't I?)

So, there you have it.

Now you know that marketing your book is actually pretty easy and very inexpensive when you use your phone. And those things you thought were holding you back? Well, you've just learned how to overcome them, so no more excuses!

Ok, it's time to take these coffee cups to the sink. (You've made me a bit self-conscious about it now, alright? I can feel you judging me.)

But, if you need more help with growing your business with video storytelling, I'm your video go-to-gal, and you can connect with me on my website: mellys.com.au

(See what I did there?)

Love and kindness always,

MellyS

everyone has a story within

GROW YOUR BUSINESS WITH VIDEO STORYTELLING

Assisting you to create video storytelling strategies that easily connect your stories with your ideal clients to sales and opportunities find you

For most people, storytelling doesn't sound very interesting. But for me, storytelling is a curiosity driven search to find the story within the heart of the people I meet.

My love for the entrepreneurial journey has led me to merge this search with assisting entrepreneurs to grow their business through video storytelling strategies. With the right connection between your stories and your clients, I believe you can develop deeper client relationships, and in the process, easily and effortlessly create sales and opportunities for you and your business.

At the core of everything I do, is a love for inspiring others to speak from the heart. I express this love by collecting and sharing entrepreneurial stories of personal growth and in doing so, I help others see the potential within themselves to find their own way to self-expression and ultimately, business freedom.

It is because of this that I am known as...

A Vision to Win

by Janice Muir

Feeling excited and in tune with being introduced on stage to present my *A Vision to Win* Book. I really wasn't sure how I was going to launch my 3rd book, and then this event crossed my path.

Get Known Be Seen. I was one of 12 women presenting on the day. My book was already 14 months old. I hadn't set a day to launch, and now here it is – June 9th, 2018.

As Trish introduced me, I had been an avid student of Trish's, and she had witnessed my growth, she had seen my hurdles and what I had achieved since working with her.

"Janice Muir is a published Author, Speaker, and online Entrepreneur…"

Introduction completed. I walked on stage to share my story.

Good afternoon, everyone. How many can remember being eight years of age?

A few hands rise.

Oh! only a couple of you? I say, and there was some chuckling over to my left; the audience was chatting amongst themselves that they couldn't remember what they did yesterday, let alone when they were eight. Laughter is a good sign when you are speaking, so you know you have engaged with the audience.

I proceeded.

I had a vision as an eight-year-old. I knew when I was in the classroom that I was going to be an author. I knew I was going to be an author, as I would write in the 3rd person for all my compositions that we did in the school. The teacher said to me one day, "Why don't you write in the first person?" I looked at the teacher. "What do you mean?" He said to me, "You're always the cat, the dog, the horse, the cow, the bird or budgie; you could be the farmer. It's never you, the person in the story. You personally sharing the journey – you're in the third person." I looked at the teacher and said, "It comes to me naturally." That is how I would write my stories in school.

45 years later, I am at a seminar. The presenter calls someone from the audience. I jumped up so quickly: "Pick me, pick me, I will do it!" "Ok!" I was there. The presenter said he had an exercise to do whilst on stage, saying, "Let's see how good you are. I'm going to throw you a bucket of balls, and I want to you to catch one of them." The presenter picked up a bucket of balls and proceeded to throw them at me.

He said, "You're up here on stage, see if you can catch one." I said back to him, "Go for it." Instantly in my mind, I am saying, "I'm going to catch a ball, only a ball in my hand; I'm going catch two balls," with determination and clarity. I was saying this to myself with vigour, "I'm going to catch a ball." This was constantly going on in my head whilst I stood on stage. And then the bucket of balls was thrown at me. I caught one in my right hand and the other one touched my middle finger on my left.

There was a lady in the first row that sniggered with a chuckle, so I leaned forward and said, "It's not funny when you are thrown a bucket of balls." The average person would shy away and put their hands up to stop the balls from hitting them, but I was determined to catch at least one. I was the presenter's first person to catch a ball. I was determined to catch a ball, and I did. A snap of fingers and the words, "Tipping point of change." That was the realization that I could do anything. It was a huge change.

A deep breath, and I moved onto the next part of my story – with only a ten-minute timeframe, I had much to fit in.

I knew that as a ten-year-old I could win in athletics. I had a vision to win. That is why this book came alive: to share the story of what the power of visualisation is all about. My gold medal is on the cover of the book: State Champion of Victoria at the age of 10 for athletics.

I wanted to go on to run in the Olympic games as a young child. I had a dream, until one person in my family said, "What makes you think you are good enough?"

I stood silent on the stage.

I never ran again.

I stood silent in front of the audience for a moment and let that absorb into their soul. Maybe one person had heard this said to them as a young child. A short silence – murmur quietness.

I share that part of my story as a way of showing that everything you want to write about comes from that passion you hold within. It comes from your heart, I said, as I touched my chest to indicate that it is all within you all inside. *It's what experience you have had in life: it's what drives you to get out of bed every morning. That's the passion you want to share in your story. A heart-felt journey.*

That's the vision you see for yourself, like Patricia sitting in the front row who spoke on being a joyous person. It's a joy inside of her, it's the drive inside of her; in fact, it's inside each of us. Each one of us has that tenacity and drive within us. We can all step into that and share our message with our story.

I took a moment to recompose myself and, realising that I was about halfway to the end of my session, I took a good breath.

45 years later, I started to write during my journey of breast cancer. I started to write about the journey I previously had about coping with losing my partner to Alzheimer's dementia. I thought that book was to be it, "This was the book that would launch me," I thought at the time. "This is it. This would be my book." However, it was not to be at the time. I have since plotted that journey coping with breast cancer alone, as I managed and coped with it on my own, and now have a book plotted with coping with losing my partner to Alzheimer's dementia. How I bring that story together, of how my partner initially was right up to the end day, is just mind blowing.

And then I realised that I have all this knowledge and personal development from what I have learned, and I can share that. I was reading as much as I could; I was gathering all this information together, and then I realised – "Oh! As a teenager, I lost my dream; oh well, I can write a book about teenagers to give them the inspiration so that they can find their own passion." And so, I bought together the book, The Well Used Key.

I held up *The Well Used Key* to the audience.

Do you know that I studied Think & Grow Rich three times? I must have been a slow learner. A large chuckle in the audience. However, after studying it three times, I got a "kaboom" moment.

I realised what the message was, so I took all that knowledge plus my own knowledge and I decided to bring a book together to inspire the teenager to find their dream, because my dream was lost.

I walked away from the audience, indicating the dream was lost.

I share with teenagers, "Don't let this happen to you, or let anyone take the dream inside of you away; whatever that passion is inside of you, is what it is for you."

This key book is the second edition. I show it to the audience. *The first edition, well ... we really don't talk about that much.* Another chuckle from the audience. *It was the first edition, it was the first experience. I dumped it out; I wrote it all on paper and went on my way to find a ghost writer, and found myself an editor who said, "You write, I will edit." That meant I would have to write, and the editor would be there supporting me all the way. So,* The Well Used Key *was born.*

After edits, restructure, layouts and typesetting were done, I needed to find a place to print. I was referred to a printing place to get a price for printing, and that was In-House Publishing on the south side of Brisbane. They printed the first book then they bought a publishing person into their establishments. They read the first book and called me in for a meeting and said, "Here is the challenge, Janice – we want you to go back and re-write the book. Add more content, give more examples, and improve on the second edition." So, I took the advice and started to go back and re-write my book. It took me over two years of tweaking, changing, putting new stuff in and improving on the first edition.

What a journey it was. I also realised how bad the first edition was. It was well worth the experience and the endurance to improve on the overall book though. I took ownership of what was said, and I took on the challenge, and I was committed to bring it into being a better book. You can download all the accessories from the book now by contacting me at JaniceMuir1957@outlook.com. The website is under re-construction; however, you can find it at janmuir.com.au.

So, whilst on this journey since breast cancer to date, I have six more books plotted:
1. The journey while coping with losing my partner to Alzheimer's Dementia;
2. Coping alone on the journey with breast cancer;
3. A series of 6 books for the younger generation on following what your passion is – 2 books done and 4 plotted; and
4. Bringing a compilation book together for 25 budding authors to share their story on their success.

One of the things that inspired me on this journey has been that I started with a printer, I moved to a publisher in the same company, then I moved on to look at an independent publishing platform, where I found Ingram Spark. Ingram Spark is what I used to publish the book A Vision to Win. I loved the journey.

I'm Janice Muir from I Believe I Achieve, and I thank you for being on this journey with me today.

Thank you. Applause, and the end of my ten-minute session.

I led a relatively quiet life until I was faced with a few of life's adversities. I was strong and gained my true strength to fight and keep the dream alive.

I have witnessed and experienced many life-changing events in my lifetime:

- Coping with partner with Alzheimer's Dementia.
- My own diverse health issues with cervical cancer and breast cancer.
- I have written 2 books to inspire teenagers to find their passion all comes from within. 6 more plots are ready to go.
- In 2012 I was retrenched from 30 years in Public service.
- 2016-17 my world opened to be an online entrepreneur.

All experiences helped to create my WHY…

- Make A Difference
- Give back with awareness
- Leave a Legacy

This chapter comes to share a journey of persistence, a journey of being focused on the end goal, and being keen to always take the next step towards said goal. This is what it takes: one step on the road to your success is achieved when you take lots of little steps to reach the goal.

My books are written to share not only to the teenager, but also to the parent, that anything you put your mind to is achievable.

I merely share to the young adult as my dream was lost as a child due to some harsh words crushing my goal.

Never give up on your own dreams; be very mindful about the words that other people say as naysayers don't believe it is possible for themselves, so they are not aware of how you can see it for yourself.

My world has changed since writing a book. I realised that there is much to accomplish in this life time and there are many people who admire a person who can bring their message to words in the form of a book. Whilst it has been part of my journey, I now offer more with a way to grow and expand myself and share a service to bring your book to life with a website that is owned by you and totally controlled by you. I inspire you to be congruent to your message find your passion, and then chat with me as I can assist you to write a book. If you don't yet know how to start, I have worked out some steps to assist along the way.

I see that your success is being in front of the industry, with all the systems automated, and able to be duplicated with ease. Being willing to learn new things and be coached to step up.

Having a different outlook to get the work done shows a true leader. In August 2017, my new path opened exactly like this. Opportunity crossed my path, and now I share a way to launch your website on line with an easy platform you can manage yourself. www.buildeasywebsites.com is one of my new outlooks to share and show a way. In 2018 I expanded again to build a platform that assists you to bring your book to life.

My book *A Vision to Win* is now available from
www.avisiontowin.com

To get your website up and running you can visit and connect with me at
JaniceMuir1957@outlook.com
or visit my site
www.builderall-janicemuir.com
for your 7-day free trial, or visit
www.buildeasywebsites.com
to download your booklet on what this arena can do for you.

My new service is taking shape at the time of this publishing and you can connect with me at Author Jan Muir on Facebook to help you get your book into life one step at a time.

https://www.facebook.com/AuthorJanMuir
or on my wall:
https://www.facebook.com/jan.muir.possum

I look forward to connecting with you.

I Believe I Achieve

Author, Speaker, Online Entrepreneur

Janice Muir
0401009778

'There are very few people in the world of retail that understand just how important the customer experience actually is. Amy Roche is one of those people. If I was a retailer, she is the only person I would call to help me create an in-store experience that translates to sales every time.'

Andrew Griffiths – International Bestselling Business Author, Speaker and Commentator

THE
RETAIL
EXPERIMENT

Five Proven Strategies to Engage & Excite Customers Through In-Store Experience

AMY ROCHE

The Retail Experiment
by Amy Roche

On the day of the Get Known Be Seen Author Expo, Amy Roche gave a compelling presentation about how her book came about and what has evolved since it was published.

Due to the success of The Retail Experiment, Amy was physically unable to write a chapter specifically for Get Known Be Seen before our gruelling deadline, so she has kindly offered a sample chapter from her book so that our readers could get an idea of what her book, and her work, is all about. We hope you enjoy her generous contribution.

UNDERSTANDING THE NEW CUSTOMER

Progress is impossible without change, and those who cannot change their minds cannot change anything.

George Bernard Shaw

Today one thing is certain: our customers (and ourselves) are savvy and way more narcissistic. It's true; unfortunately, we trust less, and we think way more about ourselves than at any previous time in history. So, it's not really a surprise that this is the so-called Age of the Consumer, is it?

Over the years, I've noticed how our customers have changed. Something that was once appreciated is now adored; what was once slightly aggravating now thoroughly angers them. Consumers today are more vocal, more emotional and way more demanding.

You've probably noticed this play out in your store too. People are getting frustrated and angered very quickly, and the smallest inconveniences turn into major dramas. Even the slightest amount of delay in, well, *anything* can set someone off.

Do you ever wonder who to blame? Are your staff inciting this type of behaviour, or are your customers just turning into a bunch of jerks? The funny thing is, it's a bit of both really. Not only are your customers changing but you and your staff are changing too – at an alarming rate.

INTENSE EMOTIONS: RISE OF STRESS AND ANXIETY IN CUSTOMERS

Yup, you heard me right – your staff and customers are changing at an alarming rate. For example:

- In any 12-month period, approximately 14 per cent of all Australians are affected by an anxiety disorder.[1]

- One in five people worldwide has recently reported increased anger and sadness, with one in three reporting stress or worry.[2]

- In Australia, 35 per cent of people report a significant level of distress in their lives.[3]

- Over 20 per cent of Americans take medications to improve their mental health.

- A 1994 survey of randomly selected households found that 15 per cent of Americans had experienced elevated anxiety the previous year. Sixteen years later this rate has risen to over 49.5 per cent.[4]

Statistics may differ from country to country, but intense and uncomfortable emotions are on the rise everywhere, and understanding customers' emotions and moods is critical for retailers. We now know emotions have a profound impact on not only how we see the world but also how we perceive products and retailers, and therefore these emotions directly affect why and how people shop and buy.

On the positive side, though, elevated levels of anxiety and anger also give people new reasons for buying – not in an icky sort of way, but more in a soothing, taking yourself to the movies kind of way. While our brains do compare value and functional benefits, and weigh up overall choices, our emotions play a large role in what we end up deciding and acting upon.

Recent brain imaging shows that both your 'worrying and computing' centre and your emotional centre are located in the same area of the brain (the ventromedial pre-frontal cortex). That means that when you are worrying about a purchase and computing value for money, the very same part of your brain is also a hotbed of emotions. This proves something smart retailers and marketers have known all along – that emotions enter and play a significant role in the appraisal and trade-off functions of buying decisions.[5]

When underlying emotions burst out

As with all things, many times what plays out in-store as crazy anger is just a case of this massive underlying anxiety mixed with poor judgement.

Let me give you an example. When I still owned my store, I heard someone getting thunderous by our front counter, so naturally, I quickly made my way to the front to see what was going on. Once there, I found a woman, let's call her Sally, who looked around 25 years old. She was extremely upset and very verbose about a $10 hair straightener that didn't work. She said it only lasted five days and then just stopped working, and she wanted to return it (she may have used other, more colourful words than that).

She was getting distraught and, as my staff stared at her in disbelief over how she was reacting to the death of the cheapest hair straightener we sold, she got even worse. We were ready to give her a new straightener, but our staff couldn't get a word in edgewise. I quickly took Sally into my office to continue the conversation where fewer customers were listening, in the hope that she would calm down.

As I talked more to Sally, I found she was upset because she had an interview that morning for what she called her dream job. Unfortunately, at the time she was living with her friend due to a recent redundancy at her last job. She had been tirelessly working to support herself and her son since her ex-partner had left and, as she said, 'This was my one shot'. Jeez, I got a little more than I bargained for on this occasion but, as Sally sat there sobbing at my desk, I couldn't help but feel for her and comfort her.

It was evident to me that she had lost the plot with our staff because she was so frustrated and stressed out over everything else going on in her life. The cheap hair straightener that didn't work was just the last straw in a series of things that had gone wrong that day, that week and really that year. And if she had walked out in that state, I think she would have blamed us for not getting the job.

Now, I know what you are thinking: *What, we're supposed to be psychologists to our customers now?* No, of course not, and I don't normally get this involved either. But we do need to recognise that our dog-eat-dog world does stress people out – to extreme states. Once in these states, they do and say things they normally wouldn't.

And this doesn't just affect your customers. To add another element to what was already a full-blown story, Jan, our customer service person who handled all of our returns – and was the most upbeat woman of all time – had had a pretty crap morning as well. Indeed, she had just been sworn at over the phone and had been fighting with the manufacturer of those *very same* cheap hair straighteners for three weeks to accept our returns. Under normal circumstances, I have no doubt she would have wooed Sally over, but on that day she was a bit flat due to her own issues and the reminder that the company we were still dealing with had yet another faulty product for her to fix up.

After talking with Sally, I realised she was clearly an educated and nice person. I explained the warranty, and said I'd be happy to give her a new unit. I also clarified that I understood her situation but didn't appreciate her taking out her frustration on my staff. She agreed, apologised profusely to Jan and everyone else and left with a smile on her face, thanking us all for our help.

I share this story because it's one in a million other retail stories, right? As owners and managers, we don't get involved in all the stories that play out throughout the day – let alone all the grumpy-bums that our lovely 'Jans' have served and soothed throughout the years. But I think this story also highlights the rise in irritability we're experiencing in our customers. And recent studies confirm that we do act differently when shopping while stressed and irritable.

In normal circumstances, in other words, when we are not stressed, we primarily use our hippocampus, which is associated with making conscious, deliberate and logical decisions. However, even when we are slightly stressed these mechanisms are thrown out the window.

Another example of this came up in my research – when staff at US-based high-end cookware and kitchen accessories store Williams-Sonoma placed a $429 breadmaker near a $279 model, they didn't sell many of the more expensive breadmakers. However, they sold double the number of the $279 model than usual.[6] This unit had always been the same price, but when placed next to the $429 unit the $279 unit seemed like a real bargain to stressed-out shoppers.

SHOPPERS' STRESS LEVELS AFFECT PURCHASES

Beyond the added stresses of life and not having the time or inclination to check prices or calculate a 30 per cent discount, other less obvious behaviours that deeply impact purchasing for stressed-out shoppers today. As outlined by consumer psychologist Kit Yarrow in *Decoding the New Consumer Mind*[7] these behaviours include the following:

- Shoppers rely more heavily on trusted experts, such as bloggers, cooking programs, friends, social sites or favourite stores that will curate excessive options for them.

- They rely more on in-store feelings to make decisions, so they are less logical and deliberate in decision-making.

- They seek human connection as an antidote for emotional distress (this will be covered in more detail in subsequent chapters).

- They are highly sensitive to complexity – if it's not simple, they are not buying. Likewise, they feel grateful and are loyal to retailers that organise and simplify the buying process for them.

- They are more prone to inertia – buying the same thing without thinking, or just not buying at all if it involves too much change.

- They are more likely to rationalise impulsive purchases. I mean, come on, who hasn't used the phrase, 'it would have cost more for me not to have bought those shoes'? This behaviour and rationalisation can be good if it's in your store, but not good if you are hoping for customers to switch from other retailers to you.

Take one tablet of control, then call me in the morning

Even anxiety, the close brother of stress, puts customers on high alert. Like its 'bro', a bit of anxiety serves to keep us safe, preparing us for that all-important 'fight or flight' mode. But Australia's Heart Foundation, and many other health organisations and practitioners warns us that prolonged anxiety can cause very negative health issues.

A retailer's 'prescription' for anxiety is control. When customers feel they have some control – even the smallest amount – they will feel less anxious. When they are less anxious, they spend more time in your store – and they also remember the positive and calm (that is, not anxious) feeling they had there. As we know, customers spending more time in-store usually means they spend more money, and having a positive psychological experience means they will come back again and again for more positive shopping experiences.

Retailers can help customers feel more in control and less anxious in-store through their verbal language (using phrases like 'it's your decision' and 'you're free to choose') and through taking the hassle out of the selection and knowledge-gathering process. I expand on these ideas throughout the book but, as a taster, great ways to streamline and curate the decision process for customers include events, how-to videos, blogs and online comparisons.

I provide more specific strategies later in this book and, obviously, you're 'free to choose' (wink, wink) which or all that may apply to your own retail environment, but you get the picture. Activating a person's sense of control makes him or her more open to persuasion.[8] This is true because that sense of control sets the anxiety and stress monster at ease. This also links in with why experts and special events featuring experts resonate so well with consumers – and are so powerful for retailers – because they give knowledge and control to the consumer.

Decision-making by committee

In *Decoding the New Consumer Mind,* Kit Yarrow makes a wonderful analogy of how we make purchasing decisions, pointing out that we often have conflicting thoughts and feelings during this process. She refers to the differing viewpoints as the 'customer's committee', arguing:

One member wants to save money, another is interested in quality, another just wants it to be a fast and an easy decision, another is focused on avoiding guilt – and then there's the fun one who's willing to do what it takes to get an emotional kick. Each committee member is vying for control. But in the purchasing moment, when emotions are in play, Mr Fast and Easy, Ms Fun, and occasionally Dr Guilt have their way.[9]

Ignoring all members in the customer's committee is the problem with traditional market research – and why so many retailers are failing as of late. The majority of retailers are still focusing on the features and benefits or price and product approach. While this 'logical' approach once attracted customers, with higher emotions now in place, it only serves a tiny portion of our customers – those who aren't anxious or emotional or stressed out. I don't know about you, but I'd be eliminated from that mix!

This approach reminds me of one of my favourite scenes from *Ferris Bueller's Day Off* – the one where the teacher is taking role call and keeps calling out 'Bueller, Bueller, Bueller', and no-one answers him. If we keep focusing on the logical side of marketing, like the teacher, no-one will answer our call either. We need to find fresh new ways to incite emotion inside our stores because most customers are already finding the logical features and benefits online, before they ever step foot in-store.

> *Without change, there is no innovation, creativity or incentive for improvement. Those who initiate change will have a better opportunity to manage the change that is inevitable.*
>
> *William Pollard*

Yes, when asked in focus groups or market research to evaluate products and anticipate what we'll do in the future, we tend to focus on product benefits and characteristics. But in the moment of purchase, we're more likely to shift our attention toward price and are much more responsive to emotional cues.[10]

This is similar to why so many people say eating healthy or being environmentally friendly is their top priority, but a small percentage act in a way that supports those statements. I wouldn't say we flat out lie; it's more that we say what we think we should say or how we would like to act, and not how we will necessarily act.

Soothe highly charged moods and anxiety

In summary, stressed and anxious shoppers can be quite difficult, but only if your store is not specially prepared for them. As retailers, we need to be very mindful of the delicate, anxious and stressed-out states of our customers. We need to have more empathy and to provide our customers with the right elements within our retail environments to make them feel at ease, connected, and to soothe their highly charged moods. Partnering with local trusted experts, providing human connection and simplifying your store to make service and purchasing easier are all ways to soothe anxiety and provide a feeling of control. I'll expand on these options in much greater detail as we progress through the book.

TECHNOLOGY AND OUR BRAINS

We all know that technology has changed us, even if we don't know exactly how. Research now shows our prolific use of technology is physically re-wiring our brains to think differently. It's also changing the way we problem-solve and creating a whole new set of emotional needs by changing our relationships and how we form them. As Kit Yarrow outlines, the cognitive and emotional shifts that result from the use of technology 'have permeated every aspect of our lives and consequently every aspect of HOW and WHY we shop and buy'.[11]

Today, faced with myriad options, consumers will choose or leave retailers because they either help to address the shifts, or fail to recognise them or ignore them.

Technology and innovations to solve all of your problems

Let me give you an example of how people now view technology and other innovations. I owned a vending machine in the foyer of our shop. I know, a crazy decision, but I made it because we were one of the first big tenants at our shopping centre. With no cafes or other big shops around, we needed a quick solution for customers and staff – otherwise, they might leave. While a vending machine is a super-annoying thing to own, maintain and stock, it did give me some great insights into our staff's drinking and snacking habits.

One of our staff, let's call him Mick, was an IT guru. He spent most of his waking hours away from work online – if he wasn't gaming, he was posting YouTube videos of gaming. However, nearly every day he had about four or five energy drinks out of my vending machine. He would stay up most of the night (or so I heard), then come to work a bit tired and in need of some stimulation. It was kinda funny because he also liked wearing a Fitbit, so he'd show his colleagues at work how little sleep he'd had, and then guzzle down some energy drink and cycle through those peaks and troughs throughout the day with coffee and snacks.

Mick told me most of his friends had energy drinks all day and also used other supplements to sleep at night. And they're not alone – rather than listening to their bodies for guidance on when they're tired or awake, Mick and his friends (and many others like them) turn to the marketplace to solve their problems. Whether this solution is a supplement, an energy drink or an app to monitor it all, as Mick told me, 'there is always an innovative solution for everything'.

More than ever before, people are looking to technology and innovations to solve their problems. In the past, a person like Mick might have realised that he was staying up too late or that perhaps all those stimulants during the day were keeping him awake at night, but not now. Mick is part of the first generation to grow up in the digital world, and he turns to the marketplace for his solutions. He and many like him want a quick fix to their problems and view innovation and technology as the go-to for product excellence. Of course, these amazing designs have also helped to create and foster a new society of super-impatient consumers.

However, without knowledge of these new psychological and sociological shifts, retailers are relying on simple historical sales data and marketing tactics, even as we know they aren't working as they once did. And it's no wonder they're not working – our consumers have changed all around us and we are still working off marketing and retailing strategies that focused on consumers long gone.

New studies are being published daily, and experts are finding more and more associations with technology – good and bad. Please don't think I'm a technophobe – I'm definitely not. I absolutely adore it. But every research corridor I went down led to more and more information on how and why consumers were changing due to technology.

It's also important to mention that while I have been cautious with the harvesting of world-class information and studies included here, by necessity we use data from the past to predict the future. With such massive changes being recorded, it simply begs the question: if we use our 'past data' to predict the 'future', how relevant will it actually be? Now, more than ever, it is a risk for retailers to assume the future is a continuation of the past.

Now, this may seem like a bit of pandemonium, but some aspects are clear. Customers are buying to satiate their heightened emotional states and to fix their problems, and are increasingly relying on technology and new innovations to do so. Knowing this, don't you want to know how and where you can help them? Wouldn't it be handy to know what motivates this new customer to shop with you regularly and to become interested in what you offer and have to say? I believe so, which is why I researched this topic for years, performed an experiment in my very own store and then decided to write a book on it all. So let's continue with our understanding of the changes in consumers so we can then focus on what we can do to combat them in-store.

ISOLATION AND OUR NEED FOR HUMAN CONNECTION

Scientists have long thought our large brains and ability for abstract thought and planning is what made the human species such a success story. But it wasn't just our big brain that helped us outfox our enemies. Neuroscience has recently discovered it was actually our ability to create large, collaborative networks, and form lasting relationships.

To improve is to change; to be perfect is to change often.

Winston Churchill

Deep human connection is our strongest motivator to succeed, learn and grow. The larger front part of the brain, our prefrontal cortex, combined with our ability to understand another human's state of mind was critical to us in those early days of forming connections. Indeed, our need to belong and connect is rooted in our very survival. In the caveman times, if you were not part of a community, you and your genes did not survive. So, in a way, everyone who is alive today has stemmed from those who learned to connect to fight, procure food and belong to a group or community.[12]

Our need to have meaningful human connection is right up there with our need for food, water and shelter. While scientists attribute human connection as being the foundation of happiness and the source of our meaning in life, we now find ourselves in a new era where the human race is becoming increasingly alone and extremely isolated.

So although we are predisposed to connection, we awkwardly find ourselves in the position of surviving alone. We are disconnecting from the very social fabric known to our genes and opting for a seemingly less anxious, less time-consuming and less interdependent social connection than ever before.

Increased isolation has been led by several shifts in society today. First off, families are no longer staying or living near each other as they once did. Secondly, our increased use of technology and social media leads to further isolation. As outlined by Gartner,

> **Nearly 60 per cent of social network users say they feel more connected to people now than they did previously. In the same exact survey, 55 per cent of them also said they have less face-to-face contact with friends, and 32 per cent said they feel lonelier now than they did previously.[13]**

Digital communication can be meaningful, but it's less intimate than face-to-face contact and, generally speaking, what we share through technology is usually more superficial in nature.

Now you may be wondering, *What the hell does isolation have to do with retailing?* Well, as I noted at the beginning of the chapter, understanding people and how they are feeling is imperative to our retail messaging and our store environments.

It seems one thing is sure: the less we interact with each other as a species, the more self-focused we become. This drives further isolation, resulting in less face-to-face time with friends and loved ones. Here are some more recent statistics in this area:

- Loneliness has doubled to 40 per cent of adults in two recent surveys, up from 20 per cent in the 1980s.[14]

- In Australia in 1975, 16 per cent of people lived alone before marriage. Skip ahead to 2013, and over 77 per cent live alone before marriage.[15]

- In an experiment conducted in 2013, people who felt isolated or excluded made riskier financial decisions and had a greater appetite for gambling.[16]

Now, as you can see, this vicious circle is not only happening in the real world with families, colleagues and individuals, but also exists in our retail world as well. As our customers withdraw from anxious situations – including pushy salespeople and oversized stores with too much choice – they begin purchasing more and more online, and become even more self-focused on satisfying their needs and wants through retailers. As we underwhelm customers on their store visits, we push them further and further away.

From our side of the situation, as retailers, we see fewer customers in-store and, in turn, we also begin focusing more and more inwardly, not on what the customer needs but what we need more of – sales. We notice that online sales erode our profit and get angry – not just with the customers but also with our own digital and e-commerce departments. Neither the retailer nor the customer is satisfied, yet neither seems ready to change; it's a Mexican standoff.

On the other hand, though, there has never been a better time in history for retailers to stand up, show their true personality and connect with their customers in a meaningful way – especially because not many are doing this. Because of this sense of isolation and the intense emotions in play, people are more prone now than ever to adore a retailer if they just reach out and connect and give back some value. Later in the book, I talk about specific strategies that help to connect and bring that human touch into your four walls of retail.

If you would like to read more of Amy's book, The Retail Experiment, *it is available at Dymocks and QBD. You can also purchase it directly from her website at*
https://retailrockstars.com.au/book/

Amy is an author, speaker and marketer with a passion for helping retailers re-connect with customers.

She's been in the marketing & retail industry in both the US and Australia for over 20 years, with global marketing experience with blue chip companies as well as owning her own Good Guys store for 11 years in Morayfield.

She's now the founding director of Retail Rockstars, which works with large multi-store retailers to develop in-store experiences and events that help to engage customers, build advocacy and drive offline and online sales.

A Writer's Journey
by Rhonda Valentine Dixon

I recognised in the early years of school that I loved language. Inserting the correct word into a sentence from a selection of words was called Blanks. Some kids groaned, but I loved Blanks. I consistently did well in English and in a couple of instances, teachers recognised my writing ability. But sadly, none took me aside to encourage me further and I was much too unaware that I could ask for direction.

In time I acquired pen pals. They were subjected to my every thought and feeling and were kind to me in their responses. Then I began to write poems. In our early teens, my dear cousin Cheryl and I retreated to her favourite place on the top of a hill in Te Horo, New Zealand. We knew that our lives would take us in different directions and as we sat immersed in the beautiful Manawatu countryside Cheryl said, "No matter where you go, don't ever stop sending me your poems." So, I sent Cheryl my poetry – until I stopped writing verse. I began writing stories instead, but I didn't own a typewriter, so another lovely friend, Christina, would type my stories for me. Christina and I went to high school together. I loved school and desperately wanted to stay and work my way to university, but, sadly education was not seen as a necessity and I had to leave at fifteen and find work.

If I documented just how many jobs I've had, you'd be forgiven for thinking I was an unreliable worker! However, this was far from the truth. I was consistently a conscientious employee. Trained as a shorthand typist, I was more comfortable in the company of animals and particularly loved being a land-girl on a dairy farm in New Zealand's Manawatu. I'd been born on NZ's railway and, in the nineteen seventies, my love of trains led me to attain a position as a stewardess on New South Wales Rail. In the eighties I gained abundant wisdom from being a London nanny. Despite wonderful successes in these and other vocations, none was a job I wanted to do forever. The one constant in my life was my writing.

At nineteen I left New Zealand to work in Australia where I wrote a little here and there, but it was when I was on the Gower Peninsula in the south of Wales that I was inspired to write my best and favourite poem. The spirit of Dylan Thomas whose boatshed in Laugharne I peeked inside on a beautiful day on the estuary thirty years after his death, was clearly within me that day.

It wasn't until I was the mother of a child with Autism Spectrum Disorder that writing became a necessity. I recognised that we, as Lin's parents, were his best advocates. I learned early in his childhood that when I wrote letters of advocacy on his behalf, they had to be devoid of emotion and in the vernacular of the Education Department to whom they were generally addressed. My goal was to attract maximum aide funding for Lin because I believed in his potential to learn. We experienced some successes and other parents began asking me for help. That prompted many letters written for families.

I learned a very important lesson from writing the first letter. A family approached me for help because staff at the school their child attended would not acknowledge the little girl even had Autism Spectrum Disorder, let alone support her. They didn't believe the mother's opinion of the child's challenges and labelled the child non-compliant, irrespective of diagnoses from several respected clinicians. The parents strongly believed the educators were failing in their duty of care. I wrote a letter that outlined all the parents' concerns and highlighted the teacher's responses to the child and actions taken by the teacher and guidance counsellor that were counterproductive to the child's ability to learn. And I named the educators. It occurred to us later that naming the educators was probably not wise. They could deny the alleged wrongdoings and take legal action against us. Thankfully, nothing dreadful for us occurred, and I learned not to be so forthcoming in naming educators in future letters. I would subsequently concentrate on the issues and suggest constructive ways to resolve them. Meanwhile, the parents moved the child to another school where she was adequately supported and where she flourished. She left high school with five academic awards and is now a successful young woman.

Stefanie Evans, Amanda Pearce, Ruth Snow, Anna Tullemans and I, all mothers of children on the autism spectrum, decided to write down what we'd learned about accessing schooling in Queensland for our children. We wanted to approach more parents than we could reach in person so that we could help them have a less than stressful experience in their advocacy journey. Schools weren't equipped to deal with such high needs kids as ours. Teachers received minimal training in ASD, if any at all, and it was clear that some schools saw autistic kids as problems rather than the unique children they were. So, in 2003 we wrote *Which School? The Questions Your Asperger Child Will Want You to Ask.* Between us we had experienced state schools, independent schools and home schooling, so we discussed all these options in the book and we gave parents ideas on how to ensure their autistic children could survive, be successfully included and potentially thrive in school. What better endorsement could we have for *Which School?* than for the foreword to be written by Professor Tony Attwood (Dr Attwood at the time)? After selling out, this resource was not reprinted due to changes in the Queensland education system – however I don't discount revisiting that project if my co-authors can be persuaded.

For the five of us, writing had also become our social life. There was abundant fun and laughter in the writing process. My love of language would have me wandering off on a wordy tangent and Stefanie would continually remind me that we had to write in "local newspaper" English for the benefit of those who experienced English as a second language or who had difficulties with literacy. Stef would laughingly chastise me for Rhondarising.

Driving home from Anna's house one day I noticed the advertising board at the Clontarf High School. It said, "Have you enrolled in uni yet?" I said out loud to no one (I was alone), "Oh, my goodness, no I haven't. I'd better do that." Going to university had been a lifelong dream but for one reason or another it had always eluded me. Our kids were still at primary school, however I recognised that no time was ever going to be the right time, so I enrolled. My husband and various good friends were consistently supportive when I needed to be at uni in out of school hours. I enrolled in a double major, Italian and Literary Studies. By the time I left university eight and a half years later with an Honours Degree in Literary Studies and a bit of a grasp on a second language, my writing had improved immeasurably.

Parents were still asking for help with advocating for their children, and they were asking for support and advice on parenting their children, so in 2002 I began writing and presenting at autism conferences. Both my husband and I advocated for families when they were too distraught to speak articulately on their child's behalf. I wrote many more letters, including on behalf of parents dealing with various other

Government Departments, including the judicial system and Child Safety.

An eighteen-year-old young lady, Maria, was in hospital, in labour with her first child when workers from the Dept. Child Safety appeared at her bedside and told her that if she took her newborn home to where her three autistic siblings lived, the baby would be taken off her. Writing as Maria, I wrote a lengthy letter. It told the Dept. how Maria felt and the impact their ruling had on her and her family. Maria complied with the Dept's. ruling because she was terrified that if she didn't her baby would be taken. It was pointless trying to reason with Dept. workers. They were simply following protocol. Maria and baby moved to an aunt's house over 60km from their own home. The difficulty with staying at the aunts was that all spare beds were occupied by overseas students. Maria and baby were welcomed and made as comfortable as possible, however it had to be on the floor and that wasn't ideal for a young woman who'd had a caesarean. Maria's mum had catered so long for the needs of all her children and tirelessly in particular for the three with autism that Maria didn't spend as much time with her mother as she wanted to. This baby was the precious gift that brought the family close together again. Maria would take her baby home to her parents' house for days at a time. A Dept. officer indicated to her that the Dept. had become aware that she was doing this. Though this revelation sounded quite menacing, the Dept. did not remove the baby from Maria's very competent care. Perhaps the letter made a difference.

When our sons were small, there was nothing available that gave them the scripts to use in everyday life, so in 2005 Anna and I wrote *How to Stop Your Words from Bumping Into Someone Else's*. This book features eighteen social stories to assist autistic children to communicate their needs in school. Prior to this, whilst in school, Lin had a small homemade book pinned to the inside of his pocket to refer to when he needed to. *How to Stop* sold in the thousands and continues to sell. I think this reflects the need for a common-sense resource that can be individualised to a specific child by parents and teachers. Though written for primary aged children, we found it was being used in high schools as well. We are currently writing a high school version.

Once again Amanda, Ruth, Anna and I devised a way of helping families. We set up No Instruction Book as a Facebook page and as a way of engaging with families and teachers in informal workshops/seminars. We took a different approach to most people who talk on autism by peppering our presentations with the poignant and amusing stories of our family lives. Family, and most importantly, living in the least stressful, most functional way, had always been uppermost in our minds.

The desire to find my extended family saw me take on a new project. In 2010, I began to search for my mother's family. Mum had no desire to be included in the search, but I wanted to know our heritage. It took five months to find them – and that alone, is an extraordinary story. When I did find them, it became abundantly clear that I needed to write the family stories down. Knowing the tragedies of the past put the present into perspective and that was empowering.

Amanda and I decided to enrol in Family History online through the University of Tasmania. This was an excellent opportunity to write those family stories and to learn to write to specific instructions in terms of word count, using dialogue and showing, not telling a story. This has been quite an emotional journey and we will complete the Family History Diploma in 2018.

In 2017 when 95-year-old Elské Winten, a fellow student in my Tai Chi class, said to me that she was so upset about losing her bamboo cane that she felt she ought to confess to her mother, I was moved and captivated. I decided that I had to write the story.

Elské doesn't need the cane to assist her with walking – she doesn't need mobility aids of any sort – people who do Tai Chi tend to have much better balance than their non-Tai Chi practicing contemporaries. Tai Chi is a discipline which is gentle on the knees but spectacular to watch when participants exercise with canes or swords. It is certainly delightful to see a class of elderly people wielding swords or walking sticks in unison. Elské's cane was eventually found, and it was a good thing that it was because it has another purpose! All is revealed at the end of the tale.

When I wrote this book, I realised it wasn't just a delightful story of an elderly lady's attachment to an old cane; it was also an excellent teaching tool. *Great-Grandma Elské's Bamboo Cane* is a multi-generational story which helps young children to understand that elderly people can do amazing things. We just need to take the time to look. In addition, it shows how a simple inexpensive everyday object, the bamboo cane, can become a lasting part of a family's tradition in a sweet and special way. If I'd thought about the fact that every word in a children's picture book needed to have impact; needed to engage little readers and hold that attention, this book might not have been written! I consulted an excellent Manuscript Appraiser, Josie Montano, who gave me valuable feedback, so I was able to make Great-Grandma the best it could be.

In 2018 I was in a mentoring session with Ocean Reeve, the publisher of *Great-Grandma* and there with us taking notes for me was Christina, the girl who'd typed my childhood stories. Once again, she was there for me, supporting my passion for writing fifty years after she'd been there for me the first time.

The Internet has made a writer's life infinitely easier. A friend of Anna's, Richard Marman, illustrated *How to Stop*. In selecting an illustrator for *Great-Grandma*, I didn't need to look any further than Richard. All the work for *Great-Grandma* was done via the internet so until the launch of the book, I'd never even met Richard.

I spent September and October 2017 in New Zealand, not only doing family history research – it was an incredible trip for that reason alone – but I was also researching another book I plan to write; the biography of a steam locomotive. This project came out of the need to write an object biography for one of the uni courses. I had to find an object that had meant something to our family. My dad had worked with this locomotive in the 1950s, so I went in search of it. With some information provided by my cousin, Murray, I found it, unrestored, rusty and raw, standing tall in a Rimutaka railway shed. It has grown greatly in my affections and I can't wait to tell its story.

I also found Cheryl on this trip back home. We'd not seen each other since that day on the hill in the Manawatu. We'd both lived in other countries, travelled widely and had families, and we'd both experienced more challenges than you could poke a stick at. But our friendship picked up exactly where it had left off a half a century before. At her home, Cheryl brought out an envelope. It contained all the poems I'd written and sent to her as a child. As I reacquainted with these treasures of my past, I reconnected with the child that I'd been. It was very special.

My journey as a writer also includes another project that I'm currently working on. It is the story of two Australian women, now in their seventies, who spent eight years in a Melbourne orphanage in the 1950's. Due to the hardship, the neglect and abuse institutionalised children often endured, they are now known as Australia's Forgotten Children and a public apology was issued to them by the then Prime Minister Kevin Rudd in 2009. These former orphanage inmates would also, in time, receive financial and psychological assistance. I am determined that these women's stories are not forgotten. We should never again make the same mistakes that were made in institutions that were meant to care.

I have another book just back from the manuscript appraiser. This will become a children's picture book – yet again with an important message evident within a poignant story. This book may be used to encourage children to play a musical instrument and I hope to engage the help of a New Zealand musical organisation to assist me to make it the best that it can be.

I'd like to encourage everyone, young and old, to write. Anyone can be a writer. You don't need to have a university degree, you just need to have a story to tell. You don't need to be concerned about spelling and grammar; there are computer programmes that will scream your errors out to you (well, not literally) and how to correct them. You don't even have to have a computer if the idea of owning one gives you the horrors; just pen and paper will suffice – and the ability to get your story down, however badly you think it might be written. If you have a desire to publish, there will be beta readers, manuscript appraisers, editors and formatters to help you to ensure your story is the best that you can make it.

If you want to write, I say, just do it. Your words could be precious or profound, revealing or reaffirming to a descendent a couple of hundred years in the future. I am fortunate to be in possession of a letter written by my great-great-grandmother to my grandfather when he was a young man. The letter tells me more about my ancestor's character than anything I've heard through family anecdote. Extraordinarily it also put into perspective some interaction I had as a fifteen-year-old with my grandfather some fifty years after the letter was written.

Don't let your story be lost to the world just because you may feel your writing isn't good enough or the story isn't worth telling. Everyone has a story and all stories are worth telling. Too many have been lost forever. Our stories can teach, inspire, encourage, enlighten, motivate, clarify, assist, entertain, challenge beliefs and bring immense joy. To leave a legacy that has the potential to do these things is an important part of the human condition. Stories set us apart from other species.

Even if you don't publish, your writing is your legacy. There is no better achievement than to have a positive impact on the life of someone else, whether it is a loved one or a stranger. But if you do publish, the sense of achievement is profound. You feel like it is your book-baby; it is your heartfelt work with your name on it. It is part of your legacy.

I can be found at the fledgling website www.rhondavalentinedixon.com where I am slowly learning to use technology. On social media I have a Facebook business page under Rhonda Valentine Dixon/Writer and a LinkedIn account. My email is rtvdixon@gmail.com and my telephone number is 0488 458 313. I welcome feedback on any of these platforms.

Rhonda Valentine Dixon

Rhonda has written since childhood. She finds it more exhilarating than anything else she does. She has an Honours Degree in Literary Studies from Griffith University and in December 2018 will complete a Diploma of Family History through the University of Tasmania.

Rhonda co-wrote *How to Stop Your Words from Bumping into Someone Else's* with Anna Tullemans. This book provides eighteen social stories to assist children with Autism Spectrum Disorder to cope in everyday life. It features one social story per page, such as 'Getting Someone's Attention', 'Starting a Conversation', 'Interrupting' and 'Asking Someone to Play' and each story may be photocopied to assist the individual child. This book has been enthusiastically received by parents and educators.

Her most recent book, *Great-Grandma Elské's Bamboo Cane*, was inspired by a delightful ninety-five-year-old woman in her Tai Chi class. Great-Grandma Elské has misplaced the cane she uses in Tai Chi. She finds it eventually, and she's very glad she does, for the cane has another special purpose. In the meantime, Elské's great-granddaughter, Harriet, learns just how amazing her great-grandma is.

This charming children's picture book (for ages 3 to 6) teaches small children that elderly people can be amazing. We just have to take the time to look.

www.rhondavalentinedixon.com

How Writing A Business Book Can Launch Your Personal Brand
by Lauren Clemett

In the 1970's it was estimated that the human brain was hit with around 500 brand messages. Today that's closer to 5,000. So, if you are feeling overwhelmed with so many brand messages confusing your brain each day, it's not surprising.

As an entrepreneur, and especially if you provide professional services where it's like selling the invisible, you have to find a way to stand out from the crowd.

There are so many ways to connect and engage with your audience, to capture the imagination of your ideal client and to encourage them to spend time and money with you.

But how do you increase the chances of them choosing you?

It's all about trust.

The brain makes decisions based on emotion and gut instinct, then uses facts to justify the purchase. You may have heard that people need to know, like and trust you before they buy from you, but in this overwhelming World, where everyone looks the same, that is truer than ever before.

That's why it's vital to create that stand-out factor as an authority in your field.

Writing a book that endorses your proficiency in your industry and is like having a really impressive business card, creating that stand-out WOW factor.

Imagine what it would be like to be introduced as an author in your field of expertise? Not only does authorship create credibility, it provides evidence that not only do you know your stuff, but that you have enough insight and expertise to fill a book.

It's important that your business book leverages your personal brand to stand out from the competition, because that's when doors really open to you.

Your book can help you get more speaking gigs. Event managers look for authors of authority, because your book is evidence that if you were on their stage you would have quality content to share.

Want to get media coverage? Journalists are incredibly time poor and work to constant deadlines, so being able to speak to an expert who knows what they are talking about and will have insight and content to help the story is ideal. Being an author is often all the evidence you need to have a journalist ask for your opinion.

The thing is, there are so many people writing books; how do you make sure your book stands out from the rest?

First, your business book needs to align with your personal brand and connect emotionally with your ideal prospect, converting them into a potential client. You may have years of experience and certainly a lifetime of experiences you have learned from, been challenged with and have used to develop your expertise. You may also have multiple careers and a lifetime of roles you may have played that can all be part of your book.

My own can include student, traveller, graphic designer, mother, entrepreneur, brand manager, award-winner …

So, what content could you use to create a stand out book that is positioning you as the go-to specialist in your industry?

What specific parts of your entrepreneurial journey do you include in your book?

Here are five key areas to focus on that not only captivate and engage the reader. They also package your natural gifts, talents and skills, along with your experience and expertise into a personal brand message that makes your book stand out from the rest.

And they are easy to remember, because you already have them in your hand…

…just hold up your fingers:

1. Thumbs Up

The first element of your book needs to convey your personal triumphs to inspire the reader and also communicate your sense of purpose and passion.

These are the things you enjoy, the things you love, the stuff you really feel at ease doing. Writing about the topics that come naturally to you, that make you feel proud. The feel-good stories that will captivate the reader. We are living in the age of the authentic brand, so sharing your real-life experiences is vital to promote your personal brand through your book.

2. Index

Your book needs to contain your area of expertise, something unique to you.

This is the things you know, perhaps from formal study or training, or they could be from the university of life. Sharing what you know is a vital part of presenting your personal brand to the World. And don't worry that you are "giving away the farm" when you share what you know. People want to know, like and trust you before they buy from you. So, sharing your value, giving people real, tangible help will ensure they want more from you.

Make them action steps, use anagrams or diagrams to help your reader remember them and recall them to others.

This is why how-to books are so appealing.

3. The Bird

Most consider telling people what you do is a vital part of promoting and marketing yourself and your business, but often a personal brand can be identified and will stand out from what you don't do.

So, make sure you include some contentious issues in your book. Uncover some dark secrets about your industry or lift the lid on processes or approaches your competitors use that you would never follow.

Every great story has a villain, and it's also vital that your reader understands that there is a purpose behind what you do, that you are a change maker and leader in your industry.

Stand up for what you believe in and be clear on what you will never condone. Help people avoid the same pitfalls you did, show them where you went wrong and what you decided you would never do again, to encourage them to trust your advice.

The brain loves a story, so share the challenges, what you learned and how the reader can apply what your experienced to ensure they don't fall into the same traps. The brain also loves to be transformed, so this is a good opportunity to use before and after style examples or case studies.

4. Ring Finger

If you want to be a well-read authority in your field, you need to engage not only the minds but also the hearts of your ideal clients. The best business books include case-studies and stories that engage the brain and have the reader wanting more from the next chapter. Consider the books you never want to put down, that you read for hours on end.

You also want to create a following and have engaging content that your "tribe" can get involved with and get behind. So, consider the types of information or activity that really agnates you. It might be innovation and following great innovators like Elon Musk or Steve Jobs, or heart-centred business and the engagement factor of Oprah.

Consider what really engages you and the content you will be interested in sharing in the long term and in social media to help promote your book.

5. Pinky

If you are writing a how-to or a business book full of awesome advice, tactile action steps and processes to help others, make sure you include all of the expertise and experience you have.

If you have been working on your area of expertise for 5 years or longer, there are so many small steps you take constantly, that you now assume everyone knows. And they don't.

Never assume people know what you know. It can be the slightest, smallest details or step that you naturally take on instinct that can save someone time and money and can transform the reader. So, don't leave these out of your book and don't underestimate the power of "common sense".

You have a totally unique approach created over your lifetime dealing with challenges, creating solutions and delivering outcomes for yourself and others. A simple way to do this is to add a foot note at the end of each chapter, or a Quick Tip section in the content.

Above all, when you write your signature personally branded business or how-to book, make sure it has your DNA stamped all over it. You have the most amazing gifts and talents that the World needs, so make sure you share them, including your personal brand story.

Be real, be you, be super helpful and be proud of what you have created.

So, what's next?

Writing a book is not actually the hard part – the promotion and marketing of the book is the hardest. I know many authors who have boxes of books in their garage!

This is why it's so important to have a personally branded book, because it makes it easier to drop it into conversation. Either networking or on email or social media, you can share your expert secrets and then provide a link to the book. You can give away a couple of chapters from your website, to encourage the reader to buy the entire book. You can use the chapters as blog posts or share the tips on podcast episodes.

There are plenty of opportunities for authors speak at live events, to be podcast guests or to provide articles on blogs and be asked for commentary by the media. You can subscribe to the Weekly Rocket to have these opportunities sent to you each week so you can rocket launch your personal brand and have your book promoted to your ideal audience around the World.

CLICK HERE for more information about the Weekly Rocket:

https://ultimatebusinesspropellor.com/weekly-rocket-2

Lauren Clemett, Personal Branding Specialist

At 8 years old, Lauren was told she had "word blindness" and would never be able to read or write properly, yet she went on to become a five-time bestselling author and International Stevie Award Winning Neurobranding expert, using her dyslexia disability as her greatest asset – helping others understand how the brain sees brands.

Lauren has over 25 years in brand management and is the owner and director of award-winning Personal Branding Consultancy, Ultimate Business Propellor, helping hundreds of entrepreneurs around the world to create stand out personal brands.

In 2017 Lauren was awarded 2017 International Women in Business Entrepreneur of The Year at the prestigious Stevie Awards in New York and regularly speaks at international summits and events.

You can find more information at www.laurenclemett.com

Who Do I Think I Am to Write A Book?

by Paula Burgess

When Trish Springsteen mentioned to me that I should write a book about my journey with my son and his Attention Deficit Hyperactivity Disorder (ADHD), I think I may have laughed in her face. Me, write a book? A girl who struggled through English at school, especially grammar and the how to express things? There was no way I was able to write a book. However, I quickly found, it wasn't about that, it was simply about getting something on paper and then an editor will fix the rest.

So, here I was, Paula Burgess, a mum of a boy who had been expelled from his day-care centre and struggling through life with a child diagnosed with ADHD and trying to run a business around this chaos. Who did I think I was, writing a book about my experiences having a child with ADHD?

Trish, who suggested I write a book told, me how easy it was. *Yeah right*, I thought. She said to me an acceptable amount of words for a book may be 30,000 words, and if I wrote 1000 words per day then I would have a book in 30 days. Now, I could do that!

So, I sat at my computer and started typing.

First though, I had to think about who I was writing this for and what I wanted from writing this book. Well, I was writing for other parents who were experiencing the same problems with their children. Their children had been diagnosed with ADHD or they suspected it was ADHD and they were feeling very alone. They were confused and frustrated with the lack of information available and they needed to find something to help them. Not only that, they needed to find someone that could not only help them, but really understood what they were going through. So, I sat and relieved my journey.

There were many times that I was typing where I was reliving the entire experience again and found myself in floods of tears barely able to focus on the words I was typing onto the screen, but this was good. It was soul cleansing, it was motivating. If I was still feeling this way even though I was through those hard times (don't worry I still have them but they are just different now), then others were too.

I continued to write until I could write no more. Doubt crept in. The wonderful self-confidence, something that I lack, made me doubt my ability to do this. Who did I think I was, writing a book to help others through their parenting challenges? Who was I to give advice on what they should do? I am not a psychologist or a parenting expert. No, but I was a parent who had lived the experience, and I just needed to write to share my own experience.

Although I knew this is my heart, it still stopped me from writing. I closed the document my book was typed on and didn't open it again for some months.

During this time, I was asked to contribute a section of the book *Parenting a Child on the Spectrum*. Again, why? Firstly, ADHD isn't officially on the spectrum as we know it; and secondly, I was just a mum. However, this book was about mum's stories, so it was perfect for me, and someone believed in me enough to ask if I would contribute.

So again, I sat at my computer and wrote my part. I hesitantly submitted it and the feedback I received was amazing.

Maybe, I do have this, maybe I can write a book after all. The document for my own book was reopened and the ideas flooded. Two weeks later I had finished my book.

That was the easy part!

Editing was next.

I hesitantly approached a school friend of mine who is an editor and asked her if she would edit my book. Lack of self-confidence raised its head again. What if she thought my writing was rubbish, what if she thought I was dumb and had no place writing a book? She said she would be happy to edit it for me and to send it through.

I sent the email and took a breath. The first email came back from her and I didn't even read it as I was too scared with what she had to say. It took all my courage to open that email to see what she had to say. She actually said to me, "You write really well Paula, your grammar sucks but the writing is great." Well, I was very relieved, and could open any further emails from her to finish the edited version of my book.

The next part was publishing. Publishing was the least of my worries with Deborah Fay beside me to assist. Deb has been with me since the beginning and encouraged me along the way that I needed to do this to help other parents in my situation. She guided me with how to start the book and what to do through the stages, even worked with my editor and graphic designer to get the book into printing form.

Honestly, without Deb I don't think I would have finished my book at all. She believed in what I was writing and how it would help other parents and gave me gentle nudges of encouragement along the way.

Then came the day that my book was edited, and I had the full transcript in my hands. Wow! What an incredible feeling!

My comfort zone had been expanded, but there was still more to do. I had to step out once again and ask two people to read this book and provide me their honest opinion. Oh dear! What if that feedback was negative? It was suggested to me to get a fellow parent and a professional to read it and give their feedback. Ok, another parent I could push myself to ask, but a professional? Now that was seriously out of my comfort zone.

I thought about this and decided that a great person to ask to provide this feedback was my son's psychiatrist. This was huge! I tentatively sat at my computer writing an email that I think I retyped about 10 times to ask her if she would read it.

She came back and said yes! Oh boy! Now I had to send it to her.

I had the book printed on A4 paper at Officeworks and had it bound, then posted it off to the psychiatrist and dropped it around to the other parent who was going to read it. That was it, it was done. I was so nervous that I nearly vomited with the thought that they were going to read this. I had to step back and remind myself why I had written this book. So many people were going to read this beyond these two people!

A few weeks later, I get an email from both of them. The other parent was first and came back and said that she loved it, it was so easy to read and she cried and laughed while completely relating to the story. She especially loved the mindset chapter at the end of the book.

Then the email from the psychiatrist came. Another email that I took ages to open, I was so nervous. She loved it! I could not believe that a woman who has studied medicine and psychiatry would love my book. She described it as a book with real stories and emotion and one that parents travelling though the same journey would greatly benefit from.

I cried! I could not believe her feedback.

It wasn't perfect, though; she did make a few suggestions to make it even better which I took on board and did as she suggested.

I then went as far as asking her to write the forward for the book, a request that she agreed to do. She wrote the most amazing forward, and I could barely read it through the tears of gratitude that I had for her.

She believed in me and what I was trying to achieve.

The book was finally ready to be sent to the printers.

Deb took care of all of that, so now was just a waiting game.

The call finally came, my proof of my book was ready!

Luckily, I only live around the corner from Deb as I was there in 5 minutes! How exciting, I was published!

However, the journey to having a book was only half done! Now I had to promote it!

First step: organising a book launch.

The venue was found, invites went out, and the book launch was held. The support I felt from my family and friends was incredible. The room I booked was actually too small for everyone that turned up, I was so surprised to see so many people there. How amazing. It was emotional but amazing, all on the same day.

Now, the work to promote the book needed to start.

How would I get this book out there?

I had a website with my business already, so of course it went up there. I promoted it across Facebook in my support groups, and sent a few media releases out, but the momentum wasn't really happening. I sold the odd book or two but nothing that best-selling author sold.

I needed another tactic; how could I use this book?

After a few meetings with my business coach we came up with the idea that we would use it as a marketing tool, and any books I sold in addition to this would be a bonus.

Again, I needed to think about my target market and who would want this book. Of course, it was parents, but who exactly? Basically, I had written this book to help parents who are going through a recent diagnosis of ADHD or suspect that their child has ADHD. My journey happened all before my son turned eight, so this was the market I needed look into.

One of my goals with my business is to become a public speaker, and it's one that I am fast becoming. I decided that speaking with day-care centres would be a great place to start. Early intervention is so important and something that has the biggest impact when it comes to an ADHD diagnosis.

Speaking to day-care centres promoting education for parents and the educators was the way to do this.

However, just sending a letter to centres was probably not going to cut it. I am sure they get many letters each day.

But hold on, I had creditability, my book! Write a book and you have creditability, it is amazing. It is like a massive business card that people don't throw away!

I send my book to every day-care centre along with a marketing letter. I followed that letter with a phone call from my office, and I ended up with a 90% success rate for the centre to agree to have me speak.

My business coach and I were amazed, results like this are rare when it comes to marketing.

Wow, a book did that!

However, the opportunities don't stop there. I received a call from 7 News after someone in their team came across a copy of my book, and they interviewed me about ADHD. Not for my book directly, but enough to give me presence as an "expert" in ADHD, which is partly what I was working for.

I was also contacted by the Herald Sun in Sydney as a result of someone coming across my book as well and interviewed me about the use of Ritalin for ADHD.

The little opportunities kept coming until one day I received a call that surprised me and put me well out of my comfort zone!

On the phone was a producer from a very well-known current affairs show. Today, I am currently unable to disclose who it was as the article has not aired to this date.

This producer had initially seen my article in the Sydney Herald Sun, checked out my website, saw my books and read my blogs, and just had to talk to me.

After chatting on the phone for about 40 minutes, he came to the conclusion that he just had to interview me and this story had to be told!

It took some time to get organised due to the sheer scale of organising that needed to be done, but in October 2017, I was officially interviewed.

When the television crew walked into my house, I was in awe at what opportunities my book had provided me. The story of the filming is another story to be told, but not in this one, and I am sure I will have a completely different and more interesting story once this story actually airs on television.

So, in a nutshell, a book has helped me grow my business and provided various media opportunities via radio, national and international podcasts, newspaper articles and television interviews.

So, why would you write a book?

Why wouldn't you?

This is just my story and the opportunities that came with it; many have other stories that have changed their life.

If you think you can't do it then you are probably limiting yourself, you probably really can.

It really is just a matter of sitting down and typing. Let it flow, don't worry about the format, layout, spelling or grammar, you can fix that later or the editor can. Just type. You may find things flow better if you actually write it rather than typing it, or you might find recording your ideas on your phone's audio recorder is a better way to process it as well. You can always get a virtual assistant to type it for you using your written papers or transcribing from an audio file.

Whatever way you need to do it, just do it.

I believe that everyone has a book in them one way or another, you just need to get started and that is the hardest part.

Remember, 1000 words per day is really not a lot, and if you continue with that outline you will have your book written within 30 days!

Believe in yourself. If you are thinking about writing a book then you can do it. Doubt will definitely creep in and you will find yourself asking why – it is important not to stop and just let things flow.

If you find that you are just blank with ideas, then take a day or two to regroup yourself by stepping away from it, and you will find that when you go back to it the ideas will start flowing again.

Enjoy the process. Your first book is a huge milestone in your life and you are likely to get the bug and write more. Trust me, I have about 10 more books in my head waiting for me to make it a priority for me to write.

What I see as one of the most important tips that I can give you when writing a book is to continually keep in mind who you are writing it for. You may start thinking about a particular market but that may actually change through the course of writing. Stop and think if your original market was who you wanted to target or is it the one you have changed the course of writing to. Maybe you have two or more books you need to write for difference markets.

Continually keep that market in your mind, and what they are going to get from reading your book.

My main aim when writing my book was that I wanted parents to be reading it and saying, "Yes, I can relate to this 100%", and to feel that they were not alone.

Another important thing to think about is how you want your book to look. I knew from the beginning that I wanted an A5 type size, but the font needed to be a decent size, so it could be read quickly.

I knew that my target market was already so overwhelmed in their life that they probably didn't actually have much time to read a book, but they wanted to so they could get the help they needed. So, I asked for my book to have a larger font than normal, and the feedback I received was that it was a very easy read and a very relatable book. I had reached both my goals with what I set out to do.

My husband never got around to reading my book himself, so I actually decided that the only way he would read it is that if I could read it to him. I did this and read it across two afternoons.

This was a fantastic way for me to realise that this book was very much an easy read both with font size and the time it took to read. The only thing I regret was that I should have recorded myself reading it to him so I could convert that to an audio book.

So, a tip for you is: if you ever go back and read your book then have your audio recorder ready and record it, then you have yourself an audio book. It's something that many people are using these days so they can listen to books while they are driving in the car.

My business has developed considerably since releasing my first book. My first book was actually *Parenting a Child on the Spectrum* which is the one I was asked to contribute to as an author amongst around 20 other parents.

Then my next book was my own, being *Beyond the ADHD Label – One Mother's Struggle for Change*.

Using these two books has given me exposure and credibility to help me grow my business.

As well as an author, I am now also a member of an Australian ADHD advocacy group and have spent 18 months studying ADHD coaching, making me an accredited ADHD coach. I run free support groups for parents of children living with ADHD. I offer education for educators, employers, recruitment agencies, day-care centres and parents about anything ADHD. I do sessions with kids, which is the highlight of my work as they are certainly world changers and have amazing personalities when they are in an environment that supports and understands them.

I have now developed a 3-week course which is based on the chapters in my book and it is sold online through my website www.beyondthemaze.com.au.

I am doing more and more public speaking to educate people about ADHD and help them understand the needs of these children. I am fast on my way to my big goal of speaking in front of thousands of people spreading the word on ADHD.

If you are reading these stories in this book then I will assume that you are considering writing a book for yourself. I cannot encourage you enough to do this.

Remember, I was terrible at English at school and had little self-confidence that I could actually write a book. Trust me: if I can write a book, you can write a book.

My biggest lesson for you is to have faith and write. Wow, that should be a meme. Seriously though, give it a go, what is the worst that can happen?

If you are a parent with a child with ADHD or a business owner with ADHD then I can help. My website has a number of blogs that will help, and free resources.

Maybe you are where I was a number of years ago where I knew that working for someone wasn't going to allow me the flexibility to be there for my son's needs and you are starting your own business; well then, you are in luck! You can use me as your support person as well! I have been there, as you will read in my book. It is a stressful but incredible journey and that I can guarantee but, trust me, you will need support. Check out my website or my book for that journey.

I have an online Facebook page: just search for *ADHD Beyond the Maze*, or you may like the online support group we have which is ADHD/ASD Support for Parents (Australia). Feel free to join that and connect with me there.

If you are interested in learning more, you can email me at info@beyondthemaze.com.au.

But wait, there's more!

I am writing more books! Told you that you would get the bug!

I am currently writing a book for parents with ADHD kids in business, a book about hard times in business and how to pull through and a book for men having ADHD kids.

Finally, my parting words for you which I have said a few times: if you are thinking about it just get it started, don't worry about the technicalities they will work themselves out in the end, just start writing, it will come. Enjoy the ride, it is amazing!

ADHD Coach Beyond the Maze

Paula Burgess is a mum of a wonderful young boy diagnosed with ADHD who changed her career path in a way she never imagined. Paula now works with parents and children affected by ADHD. She sees children with ADHD as "world changers" and works with them to help them to be the best people they can be.

Paula believes that if we teach people how to understand and accept ADHD, then it will not only open more opportunities, but it will give them permission to fly.

Paula has coached, supported and advocated for many parents of children with ADHD and worked with some wonderful children. She has given many talks to various childcare centres and conferences to educate parents on what support is available and provided educators with ideas to provide a supported classroom. She has been interviewed by various media outlets spreading the word about ADHD.

Paula is an ADDCA trained ADHD Coach and has been nominated for a variety of awards for her work with parents and children.

Her book, Beyond the ADHD Label, is designed to be to help parents who have recently received an ADHD diagnosis for their child.

www.beyondthemaze.com.au

The Accidental Author
by Di Riddell

... she found her stories mattered.

I am an accidental author. It had never crossed my mind to write a book.

Did I even have a voice? When I was a little girl, about four years of age we were at my grandparents 60th wedding celebration. It was quite a big affair and my Dad of whom I was terrified was the MC. He said something that was not true, so I stood up on my chair and corrected him right then and there. I got quite a beating over that and from incident I decided that what I had to say was not important, stay silent and you won't get into trouble, it's ok for adults to tell lies.

At that point I lost my voice and my self-worth, and I suppressed it for decades.

Come with me and let's start with milestones. My background was nursing and writing, especially creative writing, was not part of my job description. In the 1960s we were run off our feet, and for a nurse to stop and think – well, that was unthinkable. And be creative? Goodness me, that was a fate worse than death.

Then forty years ago I joined Toastmasters, a communication and leadership organisation, and began writing speeches. Most of those were five-to-seven-minute presentations, so that did not add up to committed writing either. It did, however, engender a love of the written word. I was not only finding my voice but finding that I was being listened to.

Reading has always been a passion of mine. As a child, my delight was to be curled up in my PJ's on my mum's lap as she read to me. Those stories took me to magic, fun and happy places where I forgot my troubled world. As I grew older, words and stories ignited my imagination. Over time, I got to see the world through perspectives other than my own, and it left me in awe and wonder of the marvels of the human spirit.

I got to love the characters and live momentarily in their lives. To put myself in their "for instance". Reading took me to places I had not contemplated – it allowed me to lead life vicariously through others' stories.

In 2002, the happy, secure world I knew ceased to exist. My beautiful husband of 31 years left for the heavenly fields and I was left ill-equipped to cope. I was terrified of being alone, terrified what would happen, terrified of facing a new life. So, I did what I knew best, and that was to push myself until I dropped. One year later I did exactly that. At 51kgs I was a physical, emotional and spiritual wreck. Just to compound my problems, I was computer illiterate. Les had done all my computer work for me.

At my lowest point, I began journaling. It was my saviour. I went on a deep journey of healing. The kind where all my walls came down and I was faced with the raw emotion and truth of who I was and how I felt about life. It was real, raw and ugly. I had lost my life, my identity and my voice, along with my husband.

It was tough. I was facing my own vulnerabilities, and a pile of negatives you could not jump over overwhelmed me. I was seeking, seeking, to let go, to see myself in a new light and move forward. Who can Di Riddell be in this world? How do I regain my voice? What is possible for me?

My heart gradually took me to great places and I began to understand that love conquers all, and it starts with self-love.

There were serious challenges along the way that dented my confidence as I coped, handling things I had never had to handle before. I was letting myself think that my shortcomings were failures and that lessons were burdens, and I was carrying them on my own weary shoulders.

Yet, journaling and a serious move into anything about self-development took hold of me, and it took on a life of its own. My journey continues to astound me as it unfolds. About that time, I joined National Speakers, and Robyn Henderson said those magic words – "I think you have got a book in you." I looked at her aghast! Like, what???

Time to 'fess up again: I could not create or write at the computer. I would laboriously write in long hand and then type. It was confounding, my typing could not keep up with my thoughts and if I stopped to correct I would lose my train of thought. It did not stop me... by that time, I was learning more about technology, and it was not without challenge. Many times, I sat and sobbed and cried and sometimes screamed, "I love technology, technology loves me" over and over again.

My plan to write then got all muddled up with my personal story. A story that had been kept secret for 45 years. To tell it, I knew I needed to dive deeply into forgiveness for my father, who was a violent alcoholic, and the three guys who pack raped me as a teenager resulting in a pregnancy and an adoption. It was not until I reached that place that I could write openly, authentically, and from my heart.

I did not have a clue where or how to start. My process on Robyn's advice was to do a brain dump. I dedicated my spare bed downstairs for the exercise. Every time I thought of something I would write it on a post-it-note and leave it on the bed. No judging, every thought was worth a note. After about two weeks, I had exhausted that avenue.

Collation came next, sorting into piles covering topics. If I had twenty in one pile, I broke it up into two or three areas. Where I had two in a pile, I either incorporated it into another or thought it not relevant and discarded it. Each of those plies went into a plastic sleeve with the topic on the outside.

You see, when I thought I would write from the beginning, I would get blocked, not knowing quite where to start and getting hung up on every sentence, then go blank. My voice would be hushed and I was bursting to let it out.

Those plastic sleeves were my friend. When I was ready to write I would choose what I felt like writing about in that moment. That way my creative spirit was happy and words flowed freely and my typing improved.

I mean, like, how long would it take me to write by hand then type?

What was I thinking?

Where was my head?

As I wrote I looked at other styles, what they had said. But this was to be my story, in my voice, in my words. My lesson was, "When You Write the Story of Your Life, Don't Let Anyone Else Hold the Pen". My writing is real, raw, and authentic – just like me!

Once I had covered all the topics, I collated them into an order for the book then wrote the links to draw them together. The opening and closing chapters I wrote last.

Next came the editing, book cover, typesetter and publisher. And just when I thought I was done… the launch and marketing, speaking, more writing. I thought sending off the manuscript was it. *Beyond Abuse* was out there, my secret story now public knowledge.

Why would I do that? If using my voice and sharing my story can prevent another woman going through challenges like mine, then my job is done. When I found my voice and spoke out, it gave silent permission for other women to do the same.

Completing that book opened doors I had never noticed. I moved in different directions, started a support group for women who had been abused, created a six-week program for women starting over, spoke to groups and continued writing.

Let's look further: writing for the web and a blog were my next challenge. My first blog was called 'Paint the Ceiling Beige' after regaling a blogger with stories of internet dating. It was a touch of humour and it was a fun way to express and make sense of dating in maturity.

In the process of doing a promotional video for my website, I was challenged to do a book update, to answer questions I had been asked over the last 10 years. I sent the original files to a new editor, then found out she lives in New York not S.E. Qld like I thought. She came back with several areas she considered I had glossed over. I wrote on those and answered questions I had been asked. Then she suggested I add men's stories, abuse happens to men also, so I did. Men are not being heard, they too have lost a voice, and in the fallout suicide rates are increasing. To balance it we added women's stories.

My greatest surprise was when I went to incorporate that new writing into the original copy... it did not fit. I had changed that much. My voice had matured, I had moved a long way forward. We put the new material at the end of each chapter and revised the original chapters. A new first and final chapter and a new forward completed the writing.

In May 2018, *Beyond Abuse – A Recovery Guide for Men and Women in an Era of Me, and All of Us, Too* was released. In three days it was the No 1 best seller on Amazon Australia for new releases in self-help.

The day I opened the link and saw it live on Amazon, I thought, "I am ready... I am ready to begin the search for the two babies I gave up for adoption in the 1960s." Once my mind was made up, I took action immediately. My new voice is taking me to new unchartered territory. Two things have happened: I have had a reply with partial answers (that is a start) from The Government Agency that provides the dates, time, places. Secondly, I am in touch with and supported by The Post Adoption Support Agency who help with searching and emotional support.

I have been thinking about this for a long time so I am used to the idea. I am not expecting bolts of lightning or sparks of happiness in a heartbeat. I understand that these two adults may not wish to be contacted, that they may be happy in their current circumstances or that they may be angry with me. I feel I am ready to handle that if it is a rejection. If they would like to meet me then I will be delighted beyond bounds.

Regardless of the outcome, I will have fulfilled my life in a way that leaves me content and calm. I have made my peace.

What next? As an extension of my writing, I am planning a Web TV program, *Your Voice Matters with Di Riddell – believe, be seen, be heard*. To bring understanding and meaning to life not just as it is, but for what is possible. This is not just for the "abused", all women need to be heard across the spectrum.

In finding our voice, in telling our stories, it is 2018 and we are shifting humanity and raising consciousness – we are not playing "I'm going to get you, you bastard" games. We are opening to more expansive views leading to deeper conversations.

I am not done. This story is just starting, my voice is getting stronger. Abuse is not going away, despite the millions of dollars spent on it. I am asking, "How and what can we do differently?" As a catalyst for change, I am seeking answers to questions so those who are hurting badly, those who want to get through the abuse and come out the other side in one piece, or just move on, can do so.

Beyond is my focus; we already know that to experience abuse is painful – what women want is to never feel that again, but to experience love and joy. Let's focus on finding the joy in life again. My strategies are all about finding your voice and your joy and purpose after a devasting life experience. It is not focusing on the challenge but on the road map that sets you free.

Recently I was a guest speaker at a Post Adoption Support group and I shared the video of that presentation on social media. In six days it had over 1,000 views. Adoption and all it covers is touching hearts. It affects not only the birth mother and the baby. It includes the mum's parents, the adoptive parents, siblings and grandparents. There is a whole world of hidden facts, fear, shame, guilt, anger and pain to be healed.

Each time I write, I go a little deeper; each time I get up a different woman to the one who sat down. Writing my books has gone beyond the pen. It has opened up new and varied avenues. Together we can help to make the world a safer place, and I would love to say one free of abuse. Love will conquer all.

Now, who am I? I am a mature woman, passionate about women living with joy and confidence. My writing is for women who have been through life-challenging changes. For women to be empowered and seek to find love and respect. Often, they simply wish to boost or re-fire their lives. We are living in a time of massive societal changes in relationships, family, the workforce, community and consciousness and that can be overwhelming.

Women have reinvented themselves several times over, either by choice or having it thrust upon them. They are seeking something new, something deeper, something beyond – to bring greater understanding and meaning to their lives.

Women who work with me come for one on one coaching or seek a spot in my 7-day Online Challenge as they learn to be open to new and exciting possibilities in their lives. When speaking I inspire hope with real authentic stories for those in dark places and create a space for love and light and laughter to enter. To provide a platform to uplift humanity one person at a time.

My pearl of wisdom – pick up your pen and write. Your words will heal you and touch the hearts and lives of others. It is not about perfection, it is about you showing up. When you do amazing things happens, the Universe responds.

If my words resonate with you, you can learn more about me, my book, blog and programs at www.diriddell.com or email at di@diriddell.com. I would be delighted to hear from you.

Di Riddell
Confidence Beyond 50
Speaker, author, coach
Host of the Web TV program: *Your Voice Matters with Di – believe, be heard, be seen*

Speaker, writer, author in Brisbane City, Australia

Di Riddell is an inspirational speaker, coach and author. She facilitates coaching and online challenges. Di's skill lies in demonstrating how to tap into your confidence when you need it most, with specific actionable ideas you can use immediately.

Confidence is her passion, for women 50+ who have been through life-changing challenges. Having experienced challenges ranging from the miniscule to the monumental, and having her life move from survival to thrival, she understands how it feels and offers inspiration to the world.

Her book, *Beyond Abuse – A Recovery Guide for Men and Women in an Era of Me, and All of Us, Too,* is her story along with other men and women's inspirational stories.

Mob: 0409 638 248
Phone: 07 3142 4659
Email: di@diriddell.com
Web: http://www.diriddell.com
FB: www.facebook.com/confidencebeyond50

Confidence is that extraordinary energy in you that is strong, vibrant and engaging. You know it when you see it and say, "I want some of what she has got."

Creating CONFIDENT Communicators

Trish Springsteen

Leveraging Your Book
by Trish Springsteen

As an author who made every mistake with her first book, I know what it is like to have a book sitting on shelves, in boxes or hidden up on Amazon.

Writing your book is a massive undertaking and it can be enlightening, emotional and earth shattering – and that is for the author, without taking into account what your reader's reaction is.

You spend months unlocking your heart sharing your words, your expertise, your experiences, putting it down into your book. Then you are finished, you have published; you have a print copy or a digital copy and then it stops. You hadn't given much thought to what would happen afterward.

For some authors that's okay. The book was written because they wanted to get something out and they wanted a book and so the mere fact of completing and publishing is okay – they don't want to go any further on that journey. However, for others, many others, it was meant to be the start of a journey – maybe for your business, maybe for you. Only nothing happened!

So why and how should you leverage your book?

The why is to get known, be seen. You have written your book for a reason. You need to unlock your book, share it with those who need to hear your message. When you leverage your book, you stand out from those around you. Being known as an author adds to your credibility. Your book can become your business card. It can open doors for you, bring you speaking opportunities, clients, being a guest on podcasts, radio shows and even on TV shows. It can do this if you leverage your book – are you ready to unlock your book and share it with those who need to read it, to hear your words and know you? Are you ready to stand out? Are you ready to Get Known Be Seen and become an Influencer?

Let's have a look at what we're talking about when we talk about influence. What is it? What does it mean? It used to be that if you were an influencer, we were talking about celebrities, big celebrities. Media companies or organizations would contact the influencer and ask them to talk about their product because they had huge followings. The celebrity would talk about the product; the product was then being seen by their followers. Nowadays, we don't have to be quite so much a celebrity. Getting out there and being seen allows you to become an influencer.

If you have a business of any sort, a book, product or service you don't want to make it hard for people to find your business, your book, your service or your product. You want to make it easy for your customers, your clients, and your community to find you. When you become an influencer, people are going to talk about you, your book, your product, your service.

One of the ways to become an influencer is to become a subject matter expert. That's where you become an expert on your particular subject. Quite often what happens is that you may not actually realize you are subject matter expert, because you become so involved in what you are doing, writing your book!

What happens when you leverage your book? You become the "go to" person. The more you're seen, the more you share your book and your knowledge, the more your name is going to be the first that someone thinks of when asked to recommend an expert in your area of expertise. All because you started sharing and leveraging your book. You stood out and said, "Hey, I am here."

For example: when someone says, "Who do you know who is good with Facebook?" As someone who has written the best book on Facebook ever, you want your name to be the one that is mentioned and shared. You know that you're getting known and being seen and reaching your community when your name gets shared. It can take a while for that to happen, but as you slowly build your expertise, as you slowly get out there and be seen, that is what's going to happen.

If you don't stand up there and share your expertise and shine that light for people to find you, they're not going to know to put your name out there. So, you need to make it easy for people to find you. We all wrote a book for a reason. At the least you want people to read your book or for most you want to leverage that book into a business and get clients. If you want clients, you need to be known and be seen.

Don't be selfish about sharing your book. There could be one person who needs to read your book, a chapter, a paragraph even a few words that could change that person's life. If you keep your book locked and hidden away, that person may never read or hear those words.

Authors open their heart, they pour their heart and soul into their book, and then they close the book. The book is there for sale. It might be up on Amazon, it might be a print book. It could be sitting on shelves or in boxes.

You need to take that next step and unlock the book, talk about it, shout about it so people can find it and read the words they need to read. So, to me, it's a no-brainer. If you're an author, if you want to leverage that book into a new business, leverage it into new clients, you have to be known and seen.

How do you get there? You want to stand out. You need to be standing out from everybody else around you. We are all unique. You have a message that is unique because you are unique. There are a lot of authors out there – they are not you.

So, share your unique story, your unique life experiences and expertise.

Let people see the unique you, let people see who they want to connect with. Make it easy for them to find you in amongst other authors.

So, are you ready? Are your ready to stand out and be seen and for people to find you and your book?

Some of you reading this and are saying, "Yes, yes, I'm ready." Yet others are probably shaking their heads saying, "I'm not sure, I'm nervous about speaking about my book. I'm feeling overwhelmed, it all sounds too much."

Fear is often a major limiting factor – it holds you back, it can stop you from grabbing opportunities. I can just hear those reading these words thinking – If I have to stand out people will be looking at me, people will know who I am, people will see me. Yes, that's exactly right. Scary thought, I know for many. Yes, they can see you, they can find you. That's what you want.

Along with that fear of standing out there is the fear they might find out that I don't know as much as I have written. They might find out that I don't know everything. My peers might be looking at me thinking, well, where did you come up with that information? There's this fear of being successful. What happens if you do stand up and be seen and people do start to know who you are and people do come to you to find out information?

Wow. You wake up one morning and you are a success. You wrote a book. You talked about it on an online summit and people liked it. You turned that book into an online training, you did a webinar and it worked. And then that fear of success kicks in, and you realise, "That means I will have to do it again and again." Surprisingly, fear of success is one of those limiting beliefs is that hold you back.

How can you overcome those limiting beliefs? First thing you do is you step back and you think, "What is it that's stopping me?" Is it a fear of success? Is it a fear of speaking? Is it a fear of failure? What is causing your fear – sometimes it goes back to earlier in your life. You might've stood up and tried something and it didn't work. You may have had a bad experience, or you saw someone else who had a bad experience and that could be the blockage.

To move forward on your journey, you need to own your fear. Accept that it's okay to be nervous. Turn that nervous energy into positive energy which helps you to create the enthusiasm to share and speak about your book. To have those 60 seconds of insane courage to speak on video, to do a radio or TV interview or connect with people when you're speaking at a network meeting or conference.

Remember that nervous feeling with the shaking and the butterflies in the stomach is what you also feel when you're excited. So, let's turn that switch and change the mindset to, "I'm not nervous - I'm excited. I'm going to use that adrenaline to connect with my readers, to speak, to share my book, to do a video, to do an interview."

One of the things that I like to do is take a deep breath. Hold it and breathe out. I do this three times before I get up to speak, before I do a video, before I do an interview. What I am doing is filling my body with oxygen and energy ready to speak. It gives me a calming and centred feeling, and I know that I am in control. The more you put yourself out there to be known and be seen, the more you're going to become confident. You'll realize that everything you need is in your book.

Let's look at how you can leverage your book to get known and be seen.

Firstly, it takes time to build a following. Content is golden, consistency is golden. You need to plan, look outside the square and always remember to repurpose and leverage. Don't let yourself get overwhelmed with the thought of doing new content – remember you have your book and everything you need is in that book.

Think of an avalanche: it starts with just a small pebble. It starts slowly and then it builds and builds and it becomes overwhelming and massive. That's how you being known, being seen, building your following and becoming visible grows. It starts with your small steps and the actions you take to leverage your book.

These are some of the strategies you can use:

Speaking – you need to be speaking, you need to be speaking everywhere. At network meetings doing powerful introductions, doing presentations and having conversations. You need to be speaking on video, on radio, on podcasts, online.

My recommendation is to enhance your speaking skills, techniques and strategies. You don't have to be speaking always from the stage unless that's where you want to go, but you'll find that the techniques and strategies you learn on your speaking journey are going to help you be confident in all other areas.

Discover how to structure a presentation, how speak about your book, how to speak at your book launch and how to have conversations with your readers. See where you can add emotional connection to your information to connect with your audience, your readers, and your potential clients. Learn how to harness the passion and the words you used in writing your book to speak and connect with those who need to hear your message.

Network and Listen: listen to what your readers are saying. Listen to what people are speaking about. Go to network meetings, listen to what's going on around you, make those connections and share your book. Attend conferences, get together with fellow authors and help them share their books – make it a Win-Win. Know your niche, your readers and your audience. If you don't know your niche, you don't know your audience, you don't know your readers, then you don't know who you're needing to connect with.

Networking can be physical – seek out the various network meetings. Find the ones that resonate with you and be consistent. You can also network online. Join groups on Facebook or on LinkedIn. Don't overwhelm yourself with networking. Pick the groups that resonate with you, your message and your book. Pick the ones where you're going to be finding your community. Choose two or three, if you can, personal networking groups around your area and do some online.

Your speaking skills will come in handy at the network meetings, especially when you have to get up and do your introduction. You don't want to become a name, rank and serial number. What do I mean by name, rank and serial number? You know them – the people who get up and say, "Hi, I'm Phyllis. I'm a bookkeeper. I'll do your tax returns. I'll look after your accounts, call me." And then the next person will get up and say, "Hi, I'm John. I'm a bookkeeper. I'll look after your tax returns. I'll look after your accounts, call me." And so on. Name, rank, serial number, one after the other. Are you going to remember them? No, they blur into that group of bookkeepers.

Don't become one of that blurred group of authors. "Hi – I've written a book, I'm an author – buy my book."

You want to avoid, name, rank, serial number, so that means that you need to make your introductions powerful, concise and memorable. You need to be standing out from the crowd so they remember you. Be known, be seen, stand out, be visible. You are unique.

Your book has everything you need – use stories from your book, share the pain and the solution, the problems you have solved.

Blogs and Articles: share parts of your book as blog posts. Take a chapter or a couple of paragraphs and create a blog post. Do the same as an article and share that article with magazines. You can do a search to find the ones that are resonating with your message.

You would need to create a powerful headline and tweak some of the content to make it relevant to the magazine theme.

Take a chapter from your book and turn it into an eBook, a checklist or a report which you can give away as a teaser for your book launch or lead generator. Again, change the title and tweak some of the words and content.

You don't have to create new content – you have it in your book. Just repurpose and leverage.

Social Media: Share your book and your message via Facebook posts, LinkedIn posts. Share on Instagram, YouTube, Pinterest. These are all options however you don't need to post on all of them. Find the one/s where your readers are, where your message can best connect, and concentrate on those.

Plan a strategy – work out your posts and set them for the month. Now before you start to worry about how you are going to create all those posts – go to your book. You have just written fifteen, thirty thousand words. All the posts you need are in your book. Take a couple of sentences and turn them into the posts.

You can even take some words – a quote from your own book, add an image and turn it into a meme.

Everything you need is in your book.

Webinars and Online Courses: Take all or part of your book and turn it into a webinar or an online course. You already have the content. Each chapter could be a module or a webinar, or if your chapters are large you could turn each chapter into an online course. Your reach is now becoming global.

Think about leveraging your book to appear in online summits – giving you another opportunity to share your message globally and be known and seen. Online summits are really good value for you to get your name out there because not only will people watch you on the summit, they can also connect with you.

Your speaking skills will help you connect with your listeners on the webinar and when you are doing the videos to include in your online courses.

Podcasts, Radio, Audio: You can leverage your book to be a guest on a podcast or radio show. Podcasters and radio hosts are always looking for guests and those who have a book to share and speak about stand out. Do some research, find out which podcasts relate to your message and approach them.

Radio could be online radio or local radio stations. Get to know the local radio station hosts. I've got a regular segment on a local radio station I do every month. I'm now building a following, and I go into the radio station to do that segment. This came from having a book and leveraging it to be known and seen. Think about how you can leverage your book. You might want to have your own radio show or podcast. It all depends how you want to leverage your book and the type of business you want to create.

There are opportunities for you to turn your book into an audio book that can go up on iTunes. Today in this busy world, people quite often like to listen to things, and they can do that and multitask a lot easier than other watching or reading. Those driving long distances, or when they're working around the house, when they're exercising, jogging, walking, they like something to listen to. So, you need to be looking at where you can be known and be seen using audio.

You can read your book and record your reading – there are some great free and cost-effective software available or you can outsource and get someone to read and record for you.

Video: Video is trending today. It is increasing, and you need to be out there. One of the reasons that videos are popular is it actually lets people see the face behind the book, behind the blog posts and the Facebook posts, behind the business. They actually get to see you. Remember we're talking about getting known and being seen, and video will most certainly do that for you.

You can do pre-recorded videos and upload them to Facebook, LinkedIn and YouTube. Facebook live is really trending now, and so is Instagram videos. You are now able to post longer than 60 second videos on Instagram. You need to make sure that your videos are mobile responsive.

You can have a YouTube channel to share your videos. You can also have a Web TV on YouTube. There are also other sites that will host Web TV. Don't get overwhelmed – you don't need to do everything. It's a matter of stepping back and thinking about it. Look at all the different opportunities that are available to you and choose the most appropriate.

Your videos can be a book review about your book or other books. Read a chapter from your book and post it. These are especially valuable when you are close to launching your book or doing a book signing. Do a Facebook live and share information from your book, create a discussion forum.

There are options where you can create a video without appearing in it. Lumen5 is online software that you can use to copy and paste parts of your book. Lumen5 then adds images and produces a video for you. You can also add music. In five minutes, you can have a quick video that showcases your book, you and your message.

You can turn your book into a slideshow using software like PowerPoint or Keynote, and then turn the slides into a video. Camtasia is one video tool you can use.

Remember to repurpose and leverage. Don't forget to download your Facebook Live videos so that you can reuse them on YouTube and LinkedIn as part of your online course.

The possibilities are endless, think outside the box – always remembering that you have all the content you need in your book.

Media: Don't forget to let the media know about your book. Put media releases out, connecting with the print and TV media. Share content from your book, share why you wrote your book, who your book can help. Talk about and leverage your book far and wide.

There are templates you can use to write a media release – remember, be consistent and follow up. Look for trending issues that you can connect your book to. This will catch the journalist's attention.

Avoid Content Overwhelm: Don't get overwhelmed plan your content marketing. Think about what you're going to do each month, take some time to plan. You might do a three, six months or twelve months calendar. Where will you blog, how often will you do a video, how often are you going to post, on what social media platform, what groups are you posting in, what network meetings are you attending, are you going to do webinars, how often, when will you put up your online course, and of course when are you going to do a media release. It doesn't matter what you choose as long as you are consistent and it is relevant to your book, your message and you.

One of the timesavers that I use is my Facebook Groups calendar. You can find yourself in a lot of Facebook groups and you want to leverage your book wisely. Most Facebook groups have different themes days. It can take a lot of your time going from one group to another wanting to post a particular item only to realise that you can't because of the them day for that group. What I have is an excel spreadsheet for the Facebook Groups I am in. On each page of the spreadsheet, I put the day of the week, Monday, Tuesday, Wednesday. Then on that page, each column lists the theme for that day. I put the Facebook group underneath that column for the theme and attach a hyperlink. I need only open my Excel spreadsheet go to the day of the week and see at one glance what the themes are for that day and what groups have those themes – click on the group and to straight to that group page on Facebook. I can do my entire group posting in fifteen minutes. Saves a lot of time!

You have written a book – don't let it languish on Amazon, on shelves or in boxes.

Use your book to Get Known Be Seen, to connect with those who need to read your book and hear your message. Don't be selfish share your book.

Believe in yourself. Believe in the knowledge that you have as a subject matter expert. Remember, content is major. It needs to be shared out there.

Think all the ways you can repurpose and leverage your book. Brainstorm what best suits your niche, your reader and your message. You don't have to do everything, but you will want to be in two or three different places and look at multiple ways to connect with your readers. Research, plan and take action. Getting a plan of action, a structure, getting a focus, and a goal will allow you to avoid content burnout and will allow you to maximize the variety of methods available to you to be known and be seen.

Contact Trish at info@trischel.com.au to receive a free Handy Resource Checklist and to book a Free Strategy Session to discuss how you can best leverage your book.

Here is a handy checklist which will assist you in leveraging your book.

Before Publishing:

1. Link up with other authors to cross promote your books

2. Post a sample chapter on your social media sites to stir up curiosity

3. Find blogs that review your book genre and ask for a review

4. Put a link to your website in the back of the book

5. Put links to your social media sites in the back of the book – Twitter/Facebook

6. Generate leads by offering a free gift for signing up to get the book – put that link in the back of the book

7. Develop a sign-up page with the free gift

8. Include a note from you in the book asking the reader to post a review on Amazon and on your website

9. Get your website ready – add a page for the book – include links to PayPal for sales

10. Check where you market is and share information with them

11. Publish a digital copy (Kindle version) at the same time as your print book – cross promote both books

12. Sign up for a mentoring programme with Trish ☺ – get ready to use your speaking skills to share our book

When Published:

13. Know you readers, your niche and who you want to reach

14. Have a book page on your website - link this page to PayPal for sales

15. Mention book on social media – Facebook/Google+ profile

16. Announce to your database

17. Add to your email signature

18. Source book launch venues

19. Enhance your speaking skills for the presentation at book launch

20. Think of who else you may want to present at the launch

21. Start planning your presentation for the book launch – what you will you say about your journey

22. Look at library connections – for book launches, book signings and to have your book listed

23. Explore places to guest blog about your book

24. Source interviews on podcasts, radio online and offline, WebTV

25. Schedule regular Facebook posts

26. Ask for reviews on Amazon – share reviews on the book page on your website

27. Add book and author details to Good Reads

28. Share your successes through your social media posts

29. Share reviews that you get in social media and thank readers for their reviews

30. Run promotions to keep the excitement up

31. Add videos to highlight your book

Multi International Award-Winning Speaker, Mentor, Coach & Author

Are you letting wonderful opportunities pass because you don't have the confidence to speak in front of groups?

Do you believe you have extensive knowledge and expertise which, if shared through speaking, effective communication and training, would result in new clients or revenue for your business?

Do you want to increase leads and close sales?
Would you like to transform your business?

Is your book sitting on shelves or in boxes?

Are you sitting behind your computer not sure how to share your subject matter expertise?

People work with me because they know I can help them leverage their business with speaking and communication skills. I am known for providing my clients with the confidence and structure to make speaking easy.

PH: 07 5220 0277
EMAIL: info@trischel.com.au
WEBSITE: www.trishspringsteen.com

www.ingramcontent.com/pod-product-compliance
Lightning Source LLC
Chambersburg PA
CBHW060504090426
42735CB00011B/2099